THE

WATCH JOBBER'S
HANDYBOOK.

THE

WATCH JOBBER'S
HANDYBOOK.

A Practical Manual

ON

CLEANING, REPAIRING & ADJUSTING:

*EMBRACING INFORMATION ON THE TOOLS, MATERIALS,
APPLIANCES AND PROCESSES EMPLOYED
IN WATCHWORK.*

BY

PAUL N. HASLUCK,

AUTHOR OF "LATHE WORK," "THE METAL TURNER'S HANDYBOOK,"
"THE WOOD TURNER'S HANDYBOOK," ETC.

With upwards of One Hundred Illustrations.
Second Edition, Revised.

Caplo Lumen

LONDON:
CROSBY LOCKWOOD AND SON,
7, STATIONERS' HALL COURT, LUDGATE HILL.
1889.

PREFACE.

THIS handbook is intended for the use of young beginners in their elementary practice with watchwork. The technical terms will be useful for reference to many who are older hands ; the technology of the horological art having been somewhat neglected till quite recently.

The early chapters embrace information on the repair and adjustment of watchwork which I wrote for the guidance of young beginners, and published intermittingly in a periodical. Several readers urged that this matter should be reproduced in book-form, and assured me that it would benefit a wide circle of young jobbers and have a large sale.

The Glossary of Terms used in Watchwork, which forms a large portion of this book, was prepared several years ago, and forms part of what was intended to be a comprehensive treatise on Practical Horology.

LONDON,   P. N. HASLUCK
March, 1887.

CONTENTS.

LIST OF ILLUSTRATIONS.

WATCH JOBBER'S HANDYBOOK.

CHAPTER I.

EARLY TIME MEASURERS AND MODERN WATCHES.

HERE can be no doubt that the measurement of time was first effected, and probably even suggested, by observing the heavenly bodies. When man first looked up to heaven the apparent course of the sun and that of the moon served to distinguish the days and months. These were the first divisions of time, and doubtless served the requirements of the age.

A natural day is the time required for the complete rotation of the earth on its axis, so as to bring the sun in the same relative position. This is technically called a solar day, during which the earth makes a little more than one absolute rotation. A sidereal day is the time occupied by the earth in accomplishing one absolute rotation. A solar day is the average length of all the solar days in a year, of which there are 365·242216, each divided into twenty-four hours. A sidereal day is 23 hours, 56 minutes, and 4 1 seconds; that is 3 minutes and nearly 56 seconds shorter than a mean solar day.

A practical method of indicating sidereal and mean time

B

with the same clock is to fix a wheel of fifty teeth to an axis revolving once in twenty-four hours. Let this wheel drive one having thirty teeth, carrying on the same axis one of one hundred and eighty-two teeth. This last wheel must drive one of two hundred and eleven teeth, having on the same axis one of a hundred and ninety-six, and let this drive a wheel having two hundred and eighty-one teeth. This last wheel will revolve once in 86164·0906 solar seconds, which is the length of a sidereal day to within five places of decimals. The error being, in fact, only about one second in two thousand years.

The sub-division of days into hours was only adopted when mechanical means were made available for measuring time. The earliest time measurers have the dial divided into twenty-four equal spaces. Once round the dial was equal to a day and a night. The Romans divided days and nights into periods of twelve hours each. The first mention of a period of time, translated by the word hour, occurs in the Bible in connection with Nebuchadnezzar's dream. The Babylonian king having recounted his vision, we read in the Book of Daniel :—" Then Daniel, whose name was Belteshazzar, was astonished for one hour." It is probable, however, that the modern hour was not meant.

The period of seven days, which we call a week, has no representative in the celestial world. Its origin is obscure, but some writers suppose it to be a perpetuation of the traditional account of the earth's creation. It is, at any rate, certain that the sub-division of seven days has been used from time immemorial.

Sundials were the first instruments used to divide the day into smaller portions of time. From observing that the sun's rays cast a shadow the sundial was probably suggested ; it is impossible to fix any date for this. China was the birthplace of such instruments; there the study of astronomy was practised upwards of two thousand years before Christ. The earliest record of sundials appears to be that made in the Book of Kings. Hezekiah, about 713 B.C., being sick, asked for a sign, the sun was set back ten degrees, as shown on the dial of King Ahaz. Pliny ascribes the invention to Anaximander, a Greek philosopher, about 550 B.C., but the dial of Ahaz is about two centuries older. The Chaldees probably used sundials, also the Egyptians who dwelt in the valley of the Nile long before the time of Abraham. Homer, 950 B.C., mentions the sun's diurnal and his annual race.

Sundials are now to be met with frequently, they show solar time and not the *mean* time that a clock would indicate. In country places where watches are seldom used, most people tell the time by the sun. Local expressions referring to the sun as the measurer of time are used in rural districts. Frequently the boy minding the herd is warned to bring home his charge by the shadow of a stick. These methods all show solar time, which only agrees with mean time four times a year.

Clepsydras, or water clocks, was the name of the next species of time measurers. These were vessels arranged for the gradual flow of water from one to another, and thus the flight of time was indicated Hour-glasses, which are similar to the common domestic articles used for timing the boiling of eggs, are a species of clepsydra in which sand is used, instead of water. Probably the ancients were aware of the fact that water runs out faster when there is a head of it, and took precautions to keep the clepsydra filled to a uniform height. Thus equal quantities flowed out in equal times. With sand this is different, dry sand will run out of a vessel at a uniform rate irrespective of the head it may have. A vessel kept constantly full of water will discharge a quantity equal to its contents in half the time necessary for it to empty itself if unreplenished.

An instrument of this kind is described by a recent writer, who says it is now in use on board the Proas of the Malayan Archipelago. It consists of a bucket, half filled with water, in which floats the half of a well-scraped cocoa-nut shell. In the bottom of this is a small hole, through which a jet of water rises and gradually fills the shell. So nicely is the size of the hole graduated to the capacity of the shell that it sinks exactly at the end of an hour. The man on watch then cries out the number of hours from sunrise, and sets the empty shell afloat again.

Plato is credited with having made a clepsydra about 370 B.C. They were introduced into Rome 157 B.C., and orators were timed by them. It appears that clepsydras, having wheels, were constructed and used about 245 B.C., and some of these time measurers possess evidence of considerable ingenuity. Ctesibius, of Alexandria, made a machine of this kind about 145 B.C., which indicated the hours, days, months, and signs of the zodiac. A system of wheel work was employed to register the cumulative effect of the water. Cæsar, on landing in Britain, 55 B.C., discovered by means of a clepsydra that the nights were of shorter duration than on the Continent. Alfred the Great used candles which were graduated and showed the lapse of time by the quantity consumed. It may be here noted that the principle of the clepsydra is now sometimes used for dividing time very minutely. The clock, sent by Haroun al Raschid, Caliph of Bagdad, who died A.D. 809, to the Emperor Charlemagne, was but an improved form of clepsydra.

Horologes, as clocks were formerly called, were next invented, but the date is undetermined. Wheelwork set in motion by weights and springs was known in the time of

Archimedes, between 287 and 212 B.C. The construction of a time measurer having a weight or spring seems to have been delayed for over a thousand years. Gerbert, afterwards Pope Sylvestus II., made a clock, A.D. 996, for Magdeberg. This clock had a weight for the motive power, and an escapement by which it was regulated. It is the first of which we have any knowledge. The oldest clock mentioned in England is one formerly fixed at Westminster, A.D. 1288. Gerbert, mentioned above, is usually credited with producing the first horologe; and from his time rapid progress was made in clockwork.

The pendulum, which is usually ascribed as the invention of Galileo Galelei, commonly known by his Christian name, early in the seventeenth century, was used six hundred years previously in the University of Cordova. It would appear that in its early days the pendulum was not used successfully, and that, up to the time of Galileo, horologes were probably regulated by means of fly-wheels or fans. An oscillating arm was substituted for the fly. This occurred in the fourteenth century.

Henry de Wyck, a German, erected a clock in 1364 for Charles V. of France. It was controlled by means of a contrivance consisting of a horizontal bar which pulsated by the action of the escapement. The speed of the pulsations was regulated by the amount of weights hung on the bar, or by their distance from the centre of oscillation. This contrivance acted much like the modern balance-wheel of a watch, without the balance spring. Such a clock was the time measurer used by Tycho Brahe, the Danish astronomer, who died in 1601, and by the astronomers of the sixteenth century. Several clocks of this kind were erected on the continent of Europe towards the end of the fourteenth century. The De Wyck vibrating arm was modified by Harris and applied to a clock in Covent Garden, London, in 1641.

Galileo, early in the seventeenth century, made observations on the isochronous oscillations of suspended bodies. In 1639 he published a small treatise embracing the subject. Ten years later his son is said to have constructed a clock with a pendulum. Christian Huyghens, a Dutch natural philosopher, about the same time designed improved mechanism for recording the vibrations of a pendulum. He also contrived the present form of motion work so as to put the minute hand and the hour hand at the same centre. Many experiments were made about this time, and Hooke (born 1635; died 1703) invented anchor pallets for clocks, which enabled long pendulums to be used. He also added a small sliding weight to the pendulum rod by which the centre of gravity could be adjusted with greater precision.

Watches were first introduced at the beginning of the sixteenth century. It is difficult, at the present day, to determine precisely the difference between or essential characteristics of watches and clocks. The first use of the word watch as applied to a time-keeper occurs in a record dated 1542 in which it is stated that Edward VI. had " Onne larum or watch of iron." If we distinguish a watch as being a portable time-keeper, perhaps the first would be the compass or pocket sun-dial used by the Chinese. If we distinguish watches as portable timekeepers actuated by a spring, Nuremberg Eggs, said to have been invented 1477, must be considered the earliest specimens. Derham, in his quaint " Artificial Clock-maker," says. " Watches strictly taken, are all such movements as show the parts of time, and clocks are such as publish it by striking on a bell," &c. But commonly the name of watch is appropriated to such as are carried in the pocket, and that of clock to the larger movements, whether they strike the hour or not. As to watches which strike the hour, they are called pocket clocks.

Peter Hale made pocket clocks at Nuremberg in 1500 and historians of the period pronounced them to be something quite new. A writer in 1511 accurately describes a striking watch and attributes the invention of it to Peter Hale, who died in 1540. These watches were called Nuremberg Eggs from the form of their cases. Purbach, a German astronomer (born 1423; died 1461), is said to have used watches in his observations.

The early watches had but one hand, showing the hours. They required winding twice a day. Originally the main-spring was a straight piece of steel; but the shape was soon modified. The inner end was bent into a hooked form and attached to the winding arbor. A ratchet wheel and click were added and the outer end of the spring was attached to one of the plates. A guard pin prevented an inordinate expansion of the main-spring. This arrangement is now used in American spring clocks.

Barrels, to contain the mainsprings, and fusees, to equalise their force, were introduced subsequently. Iron and steel were the metal first used in th emanufacture of watches; brass was employed about 1560. Fusees were used in 1525, and a catgut line served the office of the modern chain, which was invented about 1664. Watches were of an oval, or egg-shaped form, till 1610, when the present round shape became fashionable. Metal covers were then used to protect the hands and dial; glasses were introduced about 1620. From the writings of Shakespeare and Pepys it is evident that watches were in general use before 1600. The clockmakers of the City of London were incorporated by royal charter in 1631.

Robert Hooke, who is credited with the invention of the balance-spring, though the merit is hotly contended between him and Huyghens, was born in 1635. He is popularly, supposed to have first applied the balance spring about 1661 having invented it some three years previously. In 1691 he was created an M.D., and he died 1703. An inscription on a watch presented to Charles II. reads "Robt. Hooke invt. 1658 T. Tompion fecit 1675." Repeating watches were invented by Barlowe in 1676.

George Graham, who was born in 1675, made many important improvements in the then existing time measurers. Amongst his principal inventions is the compensation of pendulums. He used both the mercurial and gridiron compensation pendulums of the present day. The cylinder, or horizontal, escapement now commonly used in watches was invented by Graham. So also was the dead beat escapement for clocks, which is named after him. He died in 1751, leaving a name that will ever remain associated with the perfection of time measurers.

Large rewards were offered during the sixteenth and seventeenth centuries by the Spanish, Dutch, French and English governments for an instrument that should determine the longitude at sea within a specified degree of accuracy. These offers led to many ingenious devices with the object of producing a compensation for variations of temperature; and much ingenuity was brought to bear on the perfection of time measurers.

The Parliament of Queen Anne, in 1714, passed an Act granting the sum of £10,000 for a method of discovering the longitude to within sixty geographical miles, this sum to be increased to £15,000 if within forty miles, and the sum of £20,000 to be the prize for an instrument accurate to within thirty miles in a voyage from England to America. This prize was gained by John Harrison, with a chronometer made after thirty years of unremitting labour. This instrument was placed on board one of the king's ships, which sailed for Jamaica in 1758. On returning to Portsmouth, after an absence of five months, it showed an error of only eighteen miles, being very much within the limits of the largest prize.

John Harrison, mentioned above, was born at Foulby, near Pontefract, in Yorkshire, in 1693; he was originally a journeyman carpenter. He made many valuable improvements in instruments for measuring time. Having given considerable attention to the requirements of an instrument adapted for marine service, he proceeded to London in 1735 with a chronometer of his own construction, intended for determining the longitude, and obtained the prize. In 1764 he obtained £10,000 of the reward, and in subsequent years other sums, amounting to £24,000 in all. He died in 1776, in his eighty-third year. In the Patent Museum of the South Kensington Museum is an eight day clock made by Harrison in 1715. It strikes the hours, indicates the day of the month, and, excepting the escape wheel, all its wheels are made entirely of wood. This clock was going in 1871.

Considering the undeveloped state of skilled labour, as applied to the manufacture of such instruments, the chronometer made by Harrison was a wonderful production. The compensation balance applied to it overcame the variation in rate caused by the expansion and contraction of the ordinary balance and its spring in different temperatures. Thus a source of error, till then always present, was subjugated.

Thomas Mudge, born in Exeter, made some improvements in marine timekeepers. In 1793 Parliament voted him £2,500, in addition to £500 that he had previously received. He invented a gravity escapement for clocks, and also the lever escapement for watches. This, now universal, escapement was invented about 1780, and subsequently improvements were effected, the chief being those of Breguet, of Paris, and Roskell, of Liverpool, who patented the detached lever.

Clocks and watches were taxed in 1797, and the tax was repealed in 1798.

Thomas Earnshaw, born in 1749, improved upon the construction of the chronometer escapement. In 1803 the Board of Longitude resolved to grant him £500, on condition that he should disclose the construction of his timekeeper. The Board also recommended that an additional sum of £2,500 be asked from Parliament, to do justice to the merits of Earnshaw's case. In 1805 the long contested award was made to him.

John Arnold, a very clever watchmaker, born in 1744, made several very intricate specimens of watch-work. He simplified the chronometer escapement, patented epicycloidal teeth, and died in 1799 His son was voted a sum of £1,678 by the Board of Longitude.

The present century has seen so many improvements in the details of constructing time measurers of all kinds that it would be impossible to notice even those of practical value in a reasonable space The preceding information has been written principally for the purpose of showing the developments of the art before it arrived at its present state of perfection. Now we can find time measurers with which the hundredth part of a second can be measured, read, and registered with accuracy, ease, and certainty.

It will be well here to notice the chief characteristics of watches which are likely to come into the hands of a beginner, a knowledge of which will enable him to distinguish various kinds at a glance. Technically, watches are usually described: (1) by the material of the case, as gold or silver; (2) by their nationality, as English or foreign , (3) by the style of the case as open face, crystal, glass, hunter, half-hunter, or pair-cased; (4) by the escapements, as verge, cylinder, lever or duplex. These several characteristics belong to every watch. It is not

difficult to see whether the cases of a watch are of gold or silver
when the Hall-mark is visible and can be understood; but as
the greater portion of the watches in England are of foreign
manufacture, and frequently their cases are not Hall-marked,
some further guide is necessary. To an exprerienced eye a
bare inspection is sufficient, and the application of nitric acid,
or *aqua fortis*, will incontestably show the base metal.
However, this subject can scarcely be considered as part of
watch-work, as we have to deal only with the mechanism.

To decide the nationality of a watch is far from easy.
The superiority of English watches, which was at one time pro-
verbial, has been the cause of most persistent and ingenious
imitation on the part of foreigners, though their productions
could well afford to rely on their own merits in comparison
with our own at corresponding prices, and it is only to overcome popular prejudice that the imitation is made. In foreign
watches the cases usually open at the back or dome; whilst in
English the movement itself is jointed to the belly of the case,
and its inspection is effected by opening the bezel, and then
the movement may be lifted out at right angles to the case
by pressing the bolt with the thumb-nail. These peculiarities
are, however, by no means certain criteria.

Watches with cylinder escapements are almost invariably
foreign. Only a very few, and those very old-fashioned, have
ever been made in this country. A brass cap covering the
movement is peculiar to the English construction, though a
few foreign watches are made with spring-caps, which fly up
on pressing a spring-catch, the English having a locking
spring on the cap. The skeleton, or cock-movement, is
essentially foreign English makers usually make full-plate or
three-quarter-plate—that is to say, the top-plate of the movement is in the one case circular, having the balance-cock
screwed to its surface, whilst in the other a portion of the

plate is cut way and the balance-cock fixed to the pillar plate, this arrangement allowing the movement to be made much thinner.

A verge watch is known by its having the escape-wheel axis at right angles to the axes of the other wheels, &c., the direction of motion being altered by means of a crown wheel on the fourth pinion. A crown wheel is one in which the teeth are perpendicular to the plane of motion of the wheel, and by watchmakers it is usually termed a contrate wheel. The verge proper is the axis of the balance, a steel shaft having two pallets, which alternately engage the teeth of the escape-wheel. That this latter runs with its face in a vertical plane to the plates of the watch is probably the reason why this escapement is so named. Verge watches are always full-plate, but they are not made now, so that any which may come into our hands for repair will probably need it badly, and an old verge is perhaps the most difficult movement for a beginner to tackle successfully, though their low value makes them the most accessible for experimenting upon.

The cylinder, or horizontal watch, is recognised by having a cylinder as the axis of the balance. The escape-wheel is usually of steel, with teeth of a triangular form. Cylinder watches are made principally in Switzerland and France. They are characterised by their flatness, and are the most inexpensive to produce. Owing to the small compass into which cylinder movements can be packed, they are invariably used for the smallest specimens of horological skill. Very small flat watches for ladies' wear are all cylinders, and they will require very delicate handling by the inexperienced to guard against breakage. To a certain extent the danger of breaking pivots is lessened by each axis having a cock peculiar to itself, and entirely independent of all the other axes; cylinder movements of small calibre are always made with cocks throughout.

The lever escapement is used in all English watches of modern make. The majority of American watches are levers ; and Continental makers manufacture them very largely. This escapement is the best for all ordinary purposes for which a watch is required, and it is only to suit peculiarities that others sometimes take its place. The lever is readily seen in watches—one end connected with the axis of the balance, and the pallets embracing the escape-wheel. Thus the lever forms an intermediary, between the balance axis and the escape-wheel, which is dispensed with in the verge and the cylinder escapement. The axis on which the lever oscillates finds no corresponding part in the other escapements, and it will be at once apparent that the lever and all its accessories, including its bearings, are items which have to be provided over and above the component parts of a cylinder watch.

The peculiarities of each characteristic will be found described under its heading in the glossary.

CHAPTER II.

A WATCH MOVEMENT AND HOW TO TAKE IT APART.

ERHAPS of all mechanism that of a watch has the greatest charm for the ingenious amateur. The small ness of the pieces and the cleanliness that is indispensable in all operations connected with watch repairing, form an additional reason for its general favour amongst those of a mechanical turn of mind.

It has been said that "watch-repairing cannot be learned from books;" and undoubtedly there is a great deal of truth in the assertion; but at the same time it is almost as correct to say that watchmaking cannot be learned *without* books, for such a comprehensive knowledge, mechanical and scientific, is necessary to ensure uniform success that incessant book-study is quite as necessary as workshop tuition.

It is customary for apprentices to try their hands on a verge watch first, and there are several good reasons for following their example : amongst others, it is larger and stronger than is usually the case with watches that have the cylinder or lever escapement, more simple in its construction, and if any part should be broken, not so difficult or expensive to replace. It is therefore advisable if possible, to select a verge watch for first experiments ; and we will suppose one to be accessible which only requires *cleaning and examining*, and proceed to minutely discuss the method of doing this.

It will be unnecessary to further mention the duplex, chronometer, and some other escapements not in general use, as they are not likely to fall into the hands of a beginner for adjustment

In the main, the same method must always be followed whatever kind of watch is in hand, and these instructions must be understood to apply to every kind of watch in general use, no matter what sort of escapement it may have. Having neatly arranged the tools upon the work-board at the right hand, and placed a clean sheet of note-paper in the centre, we are quite ready to commence our task. Careful examination is the great secret of success in watch-repairing, and although there may be every reason for believing the watch to be in perfect condition, we must carefully look for any defects that might exist.

The intention is now to minutely describe the operation of taking a common verge watch to pieces and putting them together again properly, at the same time describing the tools used as they are named in connection with the work in hand, giving instructions for the manufacture of those which may be made by the beginner; and then to go on through various kinds of watches, and give instructions for effecting repairs of an ordinary nature which will come within the scope of a beginner.

The tools required for the purpose are neither numerous nor costly; a small screwdriver is, perhaps, the only special tool which is absolutely indispensable; a pocket knife having a small blade will be useful; and a pair of watchmaker's tweezers are also desirable. The movement has to be supported by its circumference whilst being taken apart, and for this purpose the watchmaker's eye-glass is generally used, though hard wood rings are made specially, and sold by most dealers in watchmakers' materials. In the absence of these however, a good substitute may be improvised by using the ring of a table-napkin.

The plates, wheels, and other parts of the movement are cleaned by brushing with a soft brush. Such brushes may be had from dealers in materials, and cost from about eightpence upwards. A piece of dry bread, or better, a lump of French chalk, is used to rub the brush on, and so free it from grease and dirt. Tissue paper is used to hold the parts of the movement whilst being brushed, and an inverted wineglass, one having the foot broken off being preferable, is used to cover over the parts which are cleaned. The articles enumerated are all that are really required for the operation of simply cleaning a watch, but to these must be added a bottle of watch oil, with which to lubricate the bearings before setting the machine in motion.

Screwdrivers can be bought for eightpence or a shilling, but one may be easily made by one having any skill in mechanical manipulation. The main shaft of the turnscrew may be made from pinion wire or any cylindrical rod of about three-sixteenths of an inch in diameter, having its surface facetted or grooved so as to afford a good grip for the fingers. The total length of the screwdriver, from the blade to the button, should be three and a half to four inches. The button is about the size of a threepenny piece, and revolves freely on a pivot at the end of the shaft, the pivot being riveted over to prevent the button falling off. The blade is similar to a bradawl in shape, and may be about one half to three quarters of an inch long. It is, of course, hardened and tempered. The screwdriver is used by the watchmaker in a very different fashion to that practised by other craftsmen. The watchmaker uses only his right hand, and placing the index finger on the button, he rolls the cylindrical shaft of the screwdriver between the thumb and the middle finger. The beginner should practise this mode of handling the tool, and cultivate a sensitive touch, so that he can *feel* exactly what he is doing. If the screwdriver slips from the slit of a screw an ugly scratch is sure to follow the path of the tool across the plate. When the shaft is made of steel the blade is usually filed down from the solid metal ; but a brass shaft fitted with a steel blade is equally good. A constant practitioner at watchwork should provide himself with three or more screwdrivers—one for general use, a small one for removing jewel screws, the heads of which are sometimes less than a sixty-fourth of an inch in diameter, and a large one, with a blade say one-eighth of an inch wide, to remove large pillar screws, &c. The screwdriver for general use may be just over one-sixteenth in width ; and this is the tool assumed to be provided.

Tweezers for watchwork are best bought. They should be quite plain, made tapering, from about half an inch wide at the closed end, to the points. Do not have those which are fancifully shaped. A good pair, made of steel, will cost about a shilling. The points should be hardened and tempered, and care must be exercised in clipping pieces of brass in them, as the steel will scratch. Brass tweezers are used in order to prevent such a mishap, but for the general run of work steel ones are preferable. The inside of the jaws are left quite smooth, and the serrated tweezers, such as are usually found in dressing-cases, are not adapted for watchwork.

An eyeglass is usually considered indispensable to the watch adjuster, though I entirely disagree with such a theory. It requires considerable practice to enable one to hold the glass properly by the skin around the eye without further assistance, and when the feat is accomplished but questionable benefit results. I strongly recommend anyone to work without an eyeglass if his eyesight is sufficiently good to enable him to see properly. With regard to the difficulty which beginners have in holding an eyeglass, it is equally easy to hold a glass of one or two inches in diameter, or any intermediate size.

C

To grip the glass press the upper edge under a slight fold of skin just by the eyebrow, and raise it upwards about a quarter of an inch; then let the lower edge of the glass fall upon the skin of the cheek under the eye, and the glass will be found firmly gripped. Time alone will render the beginner accustomed to wearing an eye-glass; and it is by no means an indispensable accomplishment.

The brush used for cleaning should be itself kept clean by brushing a piece of French chalk, such as is used for chalking billiard cues; or, failing that, a piece of very dry bread will serve the same purpose. When very dirty the brush should be washed with soap and warm water, and it must be thoroughly dried before being again used on the parts of a watch. For cleaning some parts alder pith is often used This is sold in bundles by material dealers.

The bench on which to make our first essay in watchwork may be the drawing-room table, for all the harm that will be done to it. Any firm table will do; and to prepare it for our use it is only necessary to spread a double sheet of white note paper on it near one side, and place a seat in a convenient position. With the tools and materials enumerated as essential lying within easy reach, and the watch to be operated on in the centre of the sheet of paper, now suppose the novice seated at the bench ready to commence operations on a verge watch. The first thing to be done is to get the movement out of the case. This is done differently in different makes of watches, but verge movements are invariably fixed in their cases by a joint and bolt. At a point just under the figure VI. will be found a small steel projection, forming a spring catch-bolt. Press this in (towards the centre), and the movement will be opened outwards, there being a joint at the figure XII.

The joint-pin should be pushed out before opening the

movement, and tyros should remember that the pin is always put in the joint with its smallest end towards the knuckle of the bezel, and must therefore always be pushed out in the direction of from the IX. to the III. The pin is generally pushed out with the points of the tweezers ; though a special tool made by inserting a steel pin in a handle, and called a joint-pusher. The majority of watch-jobbers, however, use the tweezers. After removing the joint-pin open the movement, and it will drop out of the case. Put the joint-pin loose inside the case, close it up, and lay on one side till the movement has to be replaced.

Removing the hands is the next process. This is sometimes done before the movement is taken from the case, and is perhaps the better plan for general adoption, as when the movement is laid on its back the balance-cock forms the most prominent point, and if any pressure is inadvertently brought to bear on the movement the verge stands a chance of being bent or broken. A pair of nippers, with their cutting jaws at an angle of about 45° with the handles, is the tool for removing the hands, but not being yet provided with such a tool we must use those that we have, and a penknife will serve the purpose almost as well as the nippers, and skilful workmen use the one or other with indifference. Take off the minute-hand first, by pressing the point of the knife-blade under the hand at the cannon pinion, and by a gentle twist prize the hand off; the screw-driver may be used in place of the knife, or the two may be used simultaneously, one on each side of the cannon pinion. The seconds-hand and hour-hand are taken off precisely similarly, extra caution being exercised with respect to the seconds-hand, as the pivot on which it is fixed is very fragile.

When the hands are off remove the dial thus :—Take off the cap and lay the movement, dial downwards, on the eye-glass, or on some annular stand which will support the dial near its edge, and allow the projecting square of the cannon pinion to go free ; then, penknife in hand, search for the feet, which come through the lower or pillar plate, holding the dial on.   There are three of them, each having a pin-hole diametrically across it : the pins are drawn out by pressing the knife-blade slightly into them quite close to the feet, and by a twist prizing the pins out.   The three pins thus removed should be put aside, and the movement and dial will come apart.

Under the dial, running quite loose on a small stud, will be found the minute-wheel, which communicates the motion of the cannon-pinion to the hour-wheel.   This minute-wheel must be looked after, or it will probably be lost, being quite free to drop off when the dial is removed.   Running loose on the cannon-pinion is the hour-wheel, to which the hour-hand is fixed, the cannon-pinion itself being fitted on the projecting arbor of the centre-wheel, quite tight, yet free to rotate. The cannon-pinion is taken off by gripping the square firmly, and then turning it backwards and forwards, all the while drawing the cannon off as much as possible.   It will soon be quite free of its arbor, and should be put with the hour and minute wheels.   This series of wheels and pinion forms collectively the "motion work," which is but very rarely out of order, and the only defect likely to come under the notice of a beginner will be that of the cannon-pinion not fitting sufficiently tight on the centre arbour.   This is remedied by placing a hair from the cleaning brush inside the cannon-pinion, and so jambing it on the arbor.   A more workman-like way of effecting the same purpose is to file, with a round file, a notch on two sides of the cannon about midway between the ends, and the burrs resulting will make the fit sufficiently tight.

The dial off, and motion work removed, next lay the movement face side downwards to unscrew the balance-cock. When the movement is in this position take care that the projecting seconds pivot, which carries the seconds-hand, does not touch anything or it may get broken   Unscrew the cock-screw, by turning it quite clear of the thread, and leave it lying in its place, then, with the tweezers, remove the cock. That is done by inserting one of the points between the plate and the foot of the cock, this latter having a small slot filed in it for the purpose.   Lift the cock bodily away from the plate and place it aside.   The lifting should be done vertically, so as to avoid bending the verge pivot, and this will leave the balance exposed, showing the balance-spring and regulator.

At this point may be found one of two kinds of regulator, one fitted to the hole in the top-plate, through which the verge passes, the other fitted to a circular groove cut in a piece of brass, usually of a highly ornamental character, fixed by screws to the upper plate.   Irrespective of the form of regulator, the first thing necessary is to mark the position of the end of the balance-spring which passes through the balance-spring stud, and is fixed in it by a brass pin.   Make a slight scratch on the watch plate at the end of the spring, so that when the watch is put together again you can be sure of repinning the spring in the same position.   Considerable care will be necessary to avoid any mishap in removing the pin which holds the balance-spring in the stud ; press out the pin by the aid of the tweezers, and by gently turning the balance get the spring clear of the stud. If the watch is not completely run down the train of wheels will commence to rotate as soon as the verge is disengaged from the escape-wheel, which, by the way, is always called 'scape-wheel by watchmakers.   So be careful in lifting out the balance, holding it with the tweezers by one of its arms near the centre, that the teeth of the scape-wheel do not get damaged.   By keeping a finger against the edge of the crown wheel whilst taking out the balance all danger will be avoided.

When the balance is out, let the watch run down to the full extent of the main-spring, and then proceed to " let down the spring." On one end of the barrel arbor will be found a steel ratchet-wheel held by a click—this is generally on the side where the dial comes ; with the screw-driver slack back the click-screw half a turn, and note the tooth of the ratchet-wheel which it engages ; with a good key on the projecting end of the barrel arbor give a slight turn towards winding the spring up, and after disengaging the click let the spring uncoil itself, at the same time notice how much it does so, which may be from one quarter to nearly a whole turn. This done, the chain will lie loose on the barrel, and this latter may be taken out by removing the " name bar " held to the top plate by two screws, and forming the bearing of the barrel arbor ; it is called the barrel bar, or more frequently the name bar, as on it is usually engraved the name of the ostensible maker. This bar off, the barrel is taken out after the chain has been unhooked from it ; the chain is then unhooked from the fusee and taken out. It will be advisable for the beginner to take especial notice of the hooks on the ends of the chain, and remember which belongs to the fusee and barrel ends respectively. The two hooks have quite a different form, that one having a peculiar, long tail belongs to the barrel. If there is any ornamental work fixed to the top-plate by screws, remove it, leaving all the screws resting in the holes from which they came, to save any confusion when putting together again.

The top-plate may now be taken off by drawing the pins from the four pillars, using the blade of the penknife, as previously explained, or the points of the tweezers, if found to be more serviceable. When the pins are out and put on one side—each one having its special place, and, as a rule, not being interchangeable—care should be taken to so arrange all the pins that their respective places will be easily known when the watch has to be got together again. Lift the top-plate gently from the pillar-plate, keeping the two as parallel as possible, so that the pivots will not be broken, taking especial care of the crown wheel, which will probably be caught by the potence-cock—that one which forms the bearing for the lower verge pivot, and also of the wheel end of the escape pinion. It is sometimes necessary to take the crown wheel from between the plates before these can be got asunder.

Carefully notice the position of each wheel of the train, so that you may have a good general idea of how they go back; then with the tweezers take out each separately, first the crown wheel, if not already out, through the circumstances named above, then the fusee, next the centre wheel, and finally the third wheel. It will be found that the wheels lie one over the other in the order named, and thus they must be taken out in that rotation. The pillar-plate will now be left bare, and the beginner will be well employed in putting the train—train is the technical name for all the wheelwork in a watch, from the fusee to the scape-wheel—back in its place, each wheel independent of the others, and thus familiarise himself with the positions of each and all.

Turning over the top-plate we find the scape-wheel still fixed to it; and the endshake should be tried, so that it may be the same when the watch is put together again. Near the edge of the plate will be found a stud having a plug fitted through it, and forming a bearing for the pivot of the scape-pinion. This plug is called the follower, and must be drawn out to release the scape-wheel. It need not be removed entirely, but sufficiently far to let the pivot fall out of its bearing. The potence-cock, previously alluded to, is removed by taking out the single screw which holds it, and then on the same plate will remain only the stopwork catch which prevents the watch from being over-wound. This is often not removed for cleaning, but the way to do so is to take out the pin on which the stop-finger is pivoted. It will, however, be advisable for beginners to leave all unnecessary work undone.

Parts which appear to be removable, but which are not or need not be disturbed, are the balance-spring stud on the face of the top plate; the stopwork, including stopwork stud, stop-finger and spring, on the underside of the same plate; the third and fourth wheels bar on the dial side of the pillar-plate, forming the bearings of the wheels named, and held by two screws, the stud on which the minute-wheel revolves; the locking bolt, which holds the movement in the case, and its spring; the corresponding joint, and, of course, the pillars, which must on no account be loosened. The names of these pieces are given so that the student at watchwork may make himself familiar with them; and having now taken our watch thoroughly apart, we must figuratively cover the pieces with bell glasses or inverted wine glasses till the chapter on Cleaning has been perused and then we will put the watch together again.

CHAPTER III.

EXAMINING, CLEANING, AND PUTTING TOGETHER.

ONSIDERING that the early chapters are addressed to those who have absolutely no experience in watch work, directions are not here given for ascertaining and correcting faults which would be quite beyond the beginner either to comprehend or rectify.

Cleaning will be the next process. This is simply done by brushing each part lightly with a clean brush till the adhering dirt, dried oil, &c., is removed. Hold the pieces in the fingers with tissue paper, and, as cleaned, put them under a glass cover; clean the whole movement. The plates, after being brushed, must have each hole cleaned out by the aid of pegwood, and every care must be taken to ensure the removal of every particle of dust, &c. No finger-marks must be allowed to stain the plates or other parts ; and the beginner will have some trouble in putting a movement together without touching the gilding with his fingers.

The wheels and pinions must be well brushed, and the leaves of the pinions thoroughly cleaned with a pointed piece of pegwood. A small piece of elder pith will be best adapted for cleaning the pivots. When the dirt and oil are removed from every piece, and the pivot holes in the plates "pegged out" until the pegwood comes out quite clean, the movement is ready for further examination. First see that the pillars are all tight in the frame, likewise the studs that secure the "brass edge" to the frame when the dial is not pinned on direct. If either of the pillars are loose, pin on the top-plate with four examining pins ; then rest the end of the pillar to be tightened upon a filing block, and carefully rivet the pillar till it is quite firm. In a similar manner the brass-edge pillars or studs may be tightened, removing the dial and pinning on the brass-edge to the pillar-plate. If either of the pin-holes are broken out, or the end of pillar broken off, it may be repaired in two ways. File off the broken end of the pillar till a little lower than the surface of the top-plate, make a centre mark and drill a deep hole with the largest drill it will safely bear, and then fit in a piece of brass wire to form a new pillar end, in which the pin-hole may be drilled. The other way is to use a smaller drill, and fit in a screw.

Proceed to try if all the wheels are tight on their pinions. Hold the pinion firmly between the smooth jaws of a pair of old pliers (or preferably a pair brass or copper lined), and see that the wheel has no movement either backwards and for-wards, or up and down. If a wheel is found to be loose, it must be fixed securely. Place the arbor in one of the holes of a pinion-stake, so that the pinion-head rests firmly upon it, and, with a half-round punch and hammer, carefully rivet the pinion until the wheel is tight and runs true and flat.

Wheels mounted upon brass collets, like the contrate-wheel in the verge movement, and the escape-wheel in the lever, required to be treated rather differently. The collet must rest firmly upon the jaws of a pair of clams, the clams being held in the vice, and then the brass rivet burred over slightly. In the case of a lever escape-wheel, great care must be exercised, or the wheel will be found out of flat, and it will not admit of being made true by the ordinary method of bumping. The best method of making it secure is to carefully fix the pinion arbor in the clams, and then use a fine, sharp-pointed punch, making two or three burrs on the rivet of the collet. By this means the wheel is rarely thrown out of flat. Ordinary flat wheels are riveted as nearly as possible true in flat, and then, if necessary, the arms of the wheel are bent to make it run perfectly flat. To do this the wheel is laid across the end of a bumping-up stake, and the crossings gently tapped with the hammer until the wheel runs true. The wheels must further be examined to see if any of the crossings are broken, or any of the teeth broken or bent. If a tooth is bent, it may frequently be prized to its proper position by the blade of a penknife, or sometimes by means of the tweezers.

If a tooth is broken off, a new tooth can be put in; but it is never advisable to put in more than one tooth at the same part of the wheel. A wheel having three or four consecutive teeth broken off should be discarded as quite unfit for service, and replaced by a new one. If any of the pivots show signs of wear, are rusty, or in any way rough or uneven, they must be carefully burnished till quite smooth and straight, and the ends properly rounded up. When all these points are attended to, put the centre-wheel in its place in the frame, and pin on the top-plate with the examining pins, and see if the centre-wheel runs flat with the pillar-plate, or, in other words, that the pinion is upright. This being done, the depths, endshakes, and pivot-holes claim attention. First, try the great wheel depth with the centre pinion, observing particularly at the same time that the fusee stands quite upright in the frame, for if it leans at all towards the barrel, most likely the chain will not run on properly, but slip up the fusee. See that the pivot-holes are right size, and endshakes correct; if not, alter as may be necessary. Try in the same manner the centre-wheel depth with the third pinion, the third wheel depth with the fourth pinion, and the fourth wheel depth with the escape pinion, taking care to observe the pivot-holes and endshakes. See, also, that the centre wheel is free of its bed and the third wheel of the pillar-plate.

To adjust the mainspring, the barrel, fusee, and centre-wheel are placed within the frame, and the top-plate pinned on. The chain is then attached to the fusee by the small hook, and to the barrel by the large hook, and wound up tight round the latter by turning the barrel arbor with a bench key. The ratchet is placed on the barrel arbor, and the spring set up about half a turn—that is, the arbor is turned round about half a turn more than is required to pull the chain tight. The adjusting rod is then secured to the winding square, and about one turn given to the fusee. The weight is then moved along the rod, until it exactly counterbalances the force of the spring. The fusee is then turned till filled with the chain, and tested to see if the mainspring exerts the same power at the last turn as it did at the first. If the last turn is found to have more power than the first, the spring is not set up enough. If, however, it shows less power at the last turn than at the first, then it is set up too much. When the correct adjustment is found a slight mark is made upon the end of the top pivot of the barrel arbor, and a corresponding one on the name-plate or top-plate, as the case may be. Another item requiring attention is the cannon-pinion, see that it does not confine the shake of the centre-wheel, and also that the cannon-pinion teeth are free of the third-wheel teeth.

The examination of the watch being concluded, with the exception of the escapement—which for the present we assume to be correct—it only remains to clean the different parts and put them together again. The greatest care must now be taken to *thoroughly* clean each piece, and keep it clean until the movement is replaced in the case.

The mainspring should be taken out of the barrel and cleaned. To get the spring out, first take the lid off the barrel by inserting the point of the tweezers in the notch which will be found at the edge of the barrel cover, and using them as a lever, with the edge of the barrel as fulcrum. The lid off, take out the barrel arbor, firstly unhooking it from the spring, then to get the spring out seize it by the centre part and draw it outwards, holding the barrel firmly the while. As soon as two or three coils are out, the remainder will fly out of themselves, and the operator should guard against damage by holding the spring in the barrel, and allowing it to come out gradually. Especial care will be necessary when the last coil comes out and the end has to be unhooked. Clean the inside of the barrel by wrapping a piece of tissue paper on the end of a stick of pegwood, and with that mop out the barrel. The spring is cleaned by drawing it between the jaws of the tweezers, which are covered with tissue paper. Thus the spring and the barrel will be cleaned of all the old oil.

To put the spring back is not a very easy job, and to explain how to do it is far more difficult. In the trade a special tool is used, called a spring winder, having a nose piece, corresponding to the barrel arbor, which is rotated by turning a handle, and so the spring is coiled up till small enough to go inside the barrel, then this is put on, and when the spring catches the barrel hook the job is done. In putting the spring in by hand, the barrel must be held in the left hand, and the outer end of the spring laid in it in such a position that the eye will catch on the hook, then by coiling the spring slightly it may be got in the barrel, a small piece at a time, the operation occupying but a few seconds to do; be careful to hold that spring inside the barrel in its place, or the whole lot is very apt to fly out. Clock springs are usually put in by hand in the way explained, and after a little practice no difficulty will be found in replacing the spring. Clean the barrel arbor, and also the holes in which it works in the lid and barrel, put it in its place, see that the hook catches the eye of the spring, and then snap on the cover; this is done with the fingers alone, or by pressing the cover against the edge of the bench. Do not forget that the friction on the barrel arbor is between it and the barrel, and not in the pivot holes of the plates, so that the oil must be applied to the barrel holes, and not to those in the plates. The spring itself should be well oiled when in the barrel; by putting two or three drops of oil on the coils, it will distribute itself all over the spring when this is wound up and uncoiled again. When the barrel is oiled, see that the spring is hooked at both ends before putting it down.

The chain is cleaned by wiping it with tissue paper, and running it round a stick of pegwood; no oil is put to the chain; when cleaned lay it out straight, ready for putting on.

The potence-cock must be well cleaned, and the dovetailed slip, which holds the endstone jewel against which the bottom verge pivot works, must be removed to allow the pivot hole to be cleaned. Before this cock is screwed into its place again put a very small quantity of oil in the verge pivot hole, as afterwards there will be no chance of getting at it. That only a small quantity of oil be used is most important, for if there is sufficient to flow on to the body of the verge it is sure to reach the bottom pallet, and from this the oil will be conveyed to the escape-wheel teeth, which must be guarded against. The escape-wheel itself must be placed in its bearings, and these have to be oiled before the pivots are put into the holes. That some of the pivot holes must be oiled whilst the movement is apart must not be forgotten by beginners, as it is quite impossible to get at some bearings when the plates are together. The oil used must be that specially prepared for watchwork and sold by material dealers. To apply the oil a very fine needle, made of brass, is used, or a pivot broach will do. A beginner usually errs in putting too much oil: in practice a small quantity is sufficient, and if more is put it runs away from its intended place, and is sure to get into some part where its presence will probably be a source of continual trouble.

The great wheel which forms part of the fusee must be lubricated, and it should be removed from the fusee arbor and properly cleaned. This is done by pushing out the pin, which is put diametrically through the fusee arbor just below the great wheel, between it and the bottom pivot. This pin holds on a steel collet which forms the flange against which the lower side of the great wheel takes its bearing, the upper side being against the base of the scroll part of the fusee; thus the wheel is free to revolve independent of the fusee. The clickwork is contained within the thickness of the fusee and great wheel, and will be seen as soon as the wheel is removed; the ratchet wheel being fixed to the fusee, and two clicks engaging in it on opposite sides, together with their springs are fixed to the upper face of the great wheel. Clean all the clickwork and re-oil it before putting the fusee together. See that the pin holding the fusee collet does not project, or it will probably foul the centre wheel. Try the clickwork to see that it acts all right before laying the fusee aside as done.

At this stage we are ready to put the watch together. The pillar-plate is the base on which the whole is built up, and this is the first piece to operate on. See that the bolt and bolt-spring are both screwed on; also the joint and any parts which may have been removed after the plates were taken asunder. This done, lay the plate on the top of the eyeglass, or on some other convenient stand, so that the centre pivot may go through freely. Have a glass at hand with which to cover the whole as required. To hold the movement a special contrivance is sold which has three jaws to clip the plate with, and this forms a convenient means of handling the movement as it is being put together. These appliances are not, however, generally used by the trade, though they are certainly very handy for a beginner.

All being ready for putting together, the first item to attend to is the oiling of the pivots which cannot be reached with the oiler after the movement is together. In the verge movement these are the foot hole of the potence, the dovetail hole, follower hole, and the pivots of the barrel arbor, on which the barrel turns, and the jewel holes in the frame which have end-stones or cover-pieces.

The first piece to be put on the pillar-plate is the wheel which lies next to it, generally the third wheel which lies in the circular cutting beneath the centre wheel; put this wheel in first, using the tweezers and holding by the pinion staff. See that the pivot is in its hole; then put in the next wheel, that is, the centre wheel; then the fusee, and finally the crown wheel. These being all in position put the top-plate on, and get the pillars into their respective holes, and then carefully and gradually get the pivots into their holes in the top-plate. In putting on the plate the fusee square will be the most prominent pivot, and the plate is put over that before it comes to the pillars. The crown wheel requires special care in handling, as several things tend to make it liable to breakage. It is so high up on its pinion that it becomes top-heavy, and so the top pivot gets away from the hole in the top-plate; the potence-cock and follower are apt to come in contact with the periphery of the wheel, and may, when the plates are brought together, break off the bottom pivot. As soon as the complete train is running in its bearings a slight pressure on the great wheel will cause the whole to rotate, and thus show that all s in running order. Now put the pins in the pillars, remembering that each pin has its special pillar, and that they are not interchangeable as a rule.

The barrel is now to be put in, and no difficulty will be found here. Place the barrel right side down in the circular opening of the top-plate; see that the arbor passes through the hole in the pillar-plate; then lay on the name-bar and fix it with its two screws. If the pins through the pillars, which are covered by the name-bar, are too long, or even project much on only one side, the name-bar cannot be screwed down; see to this as you go along. If the pins were replaced in the holes from which they were taken, the bar will fit on all right.

The chain must now be put on, and here the beginner will find a tedious job. Having the chain straightened out, hold the movement in such a position that that end of the chain on which is the barrel-hook may be passed from the fusee inside the pillar towards the barrel; get the hole in which the chain hooks in position, and hook the chain in. Now get a key on the square of the barrel; and, keeping the chain on the periphery of the barrel with the thumb, wind the chain on till the hook at the fusee end is in a convenient place for hooking: which do. Put the ratchet wheel on the barrel arbor, and set the spring up slightly by turning the barrel arbor in the direction indicated by the slope of the teeth of the ratchet wheel, and allow the click to hold the ratchet. Directly the power of the spring is felt by the chain the fusee will be made to turn, and the whole train of wheels will run round rapidly; the noise made will at once indicate this. The spring must be set up as much as necessary, which will be known by remembering how much it was set up before taking the movement apart, screw the click down firmly, and that part is done.

In verge watches it is very essential that the mainspring should be adjusted to the fusee, for the vertical escapement is so sensitive to variations of the motive force that the time indicated would vary with the force that reached the escapement. In other escapements in general use there is a kind or

D

compensation in the action of the escapement which does not exist in the verge.

The balance and verge are now to go in. Here you deal with very delicate parts. Put the verge in through the potence-cock, allowing it to fall by its own weight, then put the end of the balance-spring through the stud, and get it to project to the point which was marked when taking apart, then pin firmly with the pin used before ; when this pin is inserted see that the spring is quite flat, and take care it is not distorted when pinning. Be sure that the bottom pivot of the verge is in its hole, and then put on the cock, placing the steady-pins in first, and then adjusting the pivot into the hole As soon as the verge is in its bearings at both ends, the balance will swing freely, and by giving the movement a slight oscillatory motion, the balance will continue to swing whilst the cock is screwed on.

The watch must now be wound, to get the chain properly on to the fusee, and this must be guided as you go along to lead fairly into the groove of the fusee, or the chain may run up it, and the barrel will then have to be taken out and all the chain-winding process done over again. Once having the chain wound on the fusee, it will, as the spring runs down, uncoil itself on the barrel so as to be re-wound again correctly. The watch should now be in going order, and commence ticking ; if it does not, there is something wrong, which must be found out and corrected before proceeding further.

Then put on the motion work, next the dial, which pin with the three pins, taking care to see that these do not project too far and become foul of any going part. Put on the hands with the minute-hand at the XII , when the hour-hand points to either hour, finally put the movement in the case, which should have been previously cleaned, and the cleaning of the watch is completed, and it is ready for the wearer after being regulated to go fairly near to time.

CHAPTER IV.

REPAIRS AND ADJUSTMENT.

HAVING in the three preceding chapters fully detailed
the processes of taking to pieces, cleaning, and putting
together again, those faults most commonly found in a verge
watch will now be dealt with. It cannot be expected that a
beginner on examining a watch will be able to determine
whether certain parts are as they should be, for it is only after
practice that one becomes familiar with what is right, and can
then distinguish it from that which is wrong.

To direct a beginner to see that the depths are correct
seems to be absurd without giving particulars to enable him
to know know to recognise a correctly-pitched depth, and yet
to do this will necessitate a treatise on depthing—as watchmakers term what engineers call gearing—involving a far more
intimate knowledge of mechanics than can reasonably be
expected to be possessed by a beginner.

Again, to see that the endshake of a pinion is sufficient for
freedom, and not enough to cause any danger of some part of
the pinion, or the wheel on it, becoming foul of any adjacent
part, is not the work of many seconds to an experienced
watch-jobber; but how long a beginner would be in examining
whether the endshake was right, and whether he would, when
finished, arrive at a just conclusion, is a matter which it is
difficult to decide. The faults in which we are interested are
only those which affect the going of a watch in a sensible
manner; errors in the original design we need not trouble about

In that part forming the escapement by far the largest number of causes for stopping and variation are found, and the verge itself claims our first attention. We must treat it as forming part of a whole, and its proper proportion to the various component parts must be studied, for, though perfect in itself, the verge may be unsuited to the escape-wheel, and perhaps useless. A slight alteration will sometimes so much affect the relationship of a verge and escape-wheel that they are quite unsuited to each other, though once perfectly in accordance.

The following elements, forming the verge escapement, are all mutually dependent one on another, and must be considered as a whole as well as independent parts :—

The Opening of the Pallets.—That is, the angle at which the face of one pallet stands relatively to the face of the other. Watchmakers usually say that this opening should be a trifle more than a right angle, and the best authorities give one hundred degrees as the correct opening for practical purposes.

The Lift.—That is the angular motion of the balance during the time the escape-wheel is acting on the verge pallet. This should be about forty degrees, and on it will depend—

The Supplementary Arc of Vibration.—That is, the vibration of the balance after the lift, and dependent on the weight of balance, the freedom of its oscillation, and the power communicated during the lift. By adding the lift arc to the supplementary arc we get the entire vibration or angular motion of the balance, and this should be about half a complete revolution.

The recoil is that part of the angular motion of the balance which takes place while a tooth of the escape-wheel is against one of the verge pallets, and the balance is moving in the direction to cause the wheel to go backwards in spite of the motive power.

The pallet, which receives the impulse, requires to be of

a proper proportionate length, and this is a little more than half the space between the points of the adjacent teeth of the escape-wheel, measuring from the centre of the verge axis to the edge of the pallet. On the length of the pallet depends not only the leverage of the escape-tooth, but also the relative distance of the verge from the escape-wheel. With short pallets the impulse of lift will be given near the centre of motion of the balance, and will have less tendency to cause this to rotate, through the short leverage; whilst when the lift is given on a lever too long, the power is too effective, and controlling or regulating by means of the balance is made difficult.

The teeth of the escape-wheel must have their faces inclined to the axis, so that during the recoil that part of the verge pallet which is beyond the point of contact with the tooth shall be free. And here it may be as well to point out that the principal cause of wear on the verge pallet s is the recoil motion. Having mastered the above principles of the verge escapement, the beginner may proceed to a careful examination of it with some prospect of discovering any very palpable errors.

In the contrate-wheel depth generally occur many causes of stoppage; and when the complicated form of depthing is considered it is no wonder that through it loss of power and oftentimes stoppage occur. The contrate depth of a watch is a variety of skew-gearing, at all times difficult to manage, and is rendered all the more so on account of the small size of the parts. Thus we use a straight pinion where it should be conical, and a wheel with straight teeth which should be cut angle ways, because the escape-pinion does not lie diametrically across the contrate wheel, but on the skew to avoid the contrate pinion. Again, the verge escapement has necessarily, as we have previously shown, a considerable amount of recoil, and this in effect acts on the contrate wheel to an appreciable extent.

It is unnecessary for our present purpose to explain the peculiarities of the teeth of wheels used in various descriptions of gearing ; suffice to say that two wheels gearing together have teeth formed differently as they are drivers or driven, and the difference becomes the more marked as the relative size of the two wheels becomes greater ; and also, that a wheel and pinion have the teeth shaped very differently according as the one or other is driver ; and that when arranged to act in one way the reverse motion is only accomplished at an immense expense of power, if at all. We have seen that the contrate wheel drives the pinion under the disadvantages inherent to skew-gearing ; and, further, that the recoil of the escapement transforms the pinion into the driver ; and from these circumstances the depth of the contrate wheel is contrived in a way which a mechanician views as almost incredible ; and a most careful adjustment of this portion of the watch should be made so as to reconcile as many of the errors as possible. The lower pivot of the contrate pinion should have an end-stone to take the bearing from the shoulders of the pivot, but very seldom is this found.

Variation of the motive force materially affects the going of a verge watch, and it is therefore necessary to see that the power of the mainspring acts through the fusee so that an equal force is available from the time the spring is fully wound till it has run down. This is tested by means of an adjusting-rod, consisting of a steel rod a foot or so in length, with an arrangement at one end by which it can be fixed to the fusee square, at right angles to the axis, and pieces of brass, acting as weights, slide along the rod. The adjusting-rod is fixed to the fusee, and the sliding weights adjusted to an equilibrium with the spring when this is fully unwound ; and by winding up the watch with the adjusting-rod, the power of the spring is felt at each turn of the fusee, and the effective force of the spring is thus gauged. Suppose it is stronger at the fully wound than when nearly down, the spring is not set-up sufficiently, but each fusee requires peculiarities of the spring which it would be in vain to try to point out here. A long spring, in which only some of the central coils are utilised—by central coils is meant those which act half-way between fully down and tightly wound—is the best; but in a barrel of limited size the thickness of spring required to produce sufficient motive power often precludes the possibility of using one of any considerable length. A large portion of the power of the spring is often wasted in the uncoiling, by friction against the inside of the barrel, and of the coils one against another. By examining the barrel and spring it will be easy to perceive bright places, showing where friction occurs, and every effort should be made to eliminate, or at any rate to reduce it. Oil is put to lubricate the spring, and sometimes this gets so gummy that a lot of power is wasted through it.

When the source of power is fairly constant in its action it must be conveyed through the train of wheels to the escapement, without being subjected to the variations caused by bad depths, wide holes, and so forth; for all the trouble taken in regulating the power of the spring will be of little practical value if the train is faulty, though, of course, I do not mean to suggest that a badly-regulated power will act well through a faulty train. Every pivot-hole and pivot should be examined separately, and on their own merits; and when the latter are found to be cut or worn they should be re-polished, and any holes that are found to be wide must be re-bushed, and the pivot fitted properly. In all cases of re-bushing pivot-holes the French *bouchons*, sold by material dealers, will be found the best things to use. When a hole is out of upright, or badly pitched, and requires re-drilling, then use a piece of hard brass wire to plug the old hole with. Of the inherent bad qualities, and the special attention to be paid to the contrate depth, I have already spoken. The verge itself must run with the shoulders of its pivot free of the bearings, and the lower pallet must be sufficiently far from the potence to guard against the possibility of the oil applied to the pivot-hole coming in contact with it. For a similar reason the top pivot must be long enough, or the oil will spread on the balance or balance-spring collet, and be apt to form a sticky film between it and the balance-cock.

The balance should run true, and be in perfect equipoise when the spring is removed, and be free of the cock, the potence, and all adjacent parts. The verge pivots should be about three diameters long, and the ends should be flat, not pointed, so as to equalise the friction as much as possible when the watch is in a horizontal or vertical position. The spring must be pinned quite tight to the collet on the verge, and this must be in the exact centre of the spring. The number of turns may be from six to eight, as it is found in practice that longer springs—that is, those with more coils—do not give such good results, a circumstance which may be explained by the short arc of vibration of the verge escapement.

Setting of the balance is the result of insufficiency of the motive power, and may be caused by anything which hampers the effect of the spring, or through a weak spring, or through the pallet being at a wrong angle, so that the force is applied to it at a place and in a direction where the leverage is insufficient. The insufficiency of motive power may sometimes be caused by the excessive friction or weight of the balance, or anything which tends to make this difficult to move. Oil applied to the pallet will, when it becomes thick, very seriously impede the progress of the escape-tooth over the pallet face during the lift, and oil should not be used on the verge at all, and hence a stronger reason for seeing that the lower pallet does not gather oil from the bearing of the bottom pivot.

A verge which is itself bent, or has bent pivots, or in which these have been turned not exactly concentric with the body of the verge, will be always a source of trouble, and if the defect cannot be remedied a new verge should be put. If the escape-wheel axis is not properly at right angles with the balance axis, the action of one pallet will be deeper than that of the other, the lift greater, and the arc made on each side of the point of rest will be unequal. The above enumerate most of the defects which are the result of former injudicious alterations, or so-called repairs, and those caused by simple wear and tear.

The breakages of most frequent occurrence will now be noticed, and directions given for mending.

Broken mainsprings are perhaps the most serious and the most common of breakages. What causes springs to break has as yet not been satisfactorily explained, but probably peculiar variations in the temperature are the chief cause, as it is usual to find that a large number of springs break at the same time. This mishap is often accompanied by a broken chain, this latter being caused by the barrel running backwards on the spring pressure failing. A broken spring may be repaired, or at least used again, if the breakage has occurred near to the outer end, and the length of the spring not much shortened by the piece broken. It is then only necessary to soften the extreme end of the spring, and punch a hole in it to hook on to the pin projecting inside the barrels. After trimming off the broken edge smoothly, the spring is put back in its place, and usually will be as good as a new one. If a new one has to be put, it should be selected as nearly as possible of the same strength as the old one, and, of course, of the same width. Put the new spring in the barrel, and notice its length, or how much of the space it occupies. The proper proportion is this : the space of the arbor in the centre to the side of the barrel should be equally divided, and one half occupied by the spring. On the supposition that the old spring was correct for strength, it should always be replaced with one as nearly as possible like it. If the spring occupies more than half the space, take it out and break off a piece till the proper length is attained ; now heat half an inch of the end not quite red hot, punch a round hole about three-eighths of an inch from the end, then taper off the point of the spring, leaving it full width where the hole is. Some watches have the mainspring hook riveted to the barrel, and some to the spring. If the former, you will have no trouble but to make the hole in your spring large enough to hook on ; if you have to rivet the hook to the spring you may be able to make use of the old one.

Suppose that we have a broken spring to replace, which evidently is not of the proper width and strength for the barrel it occupied, and consequently not adapted to the watch. The first consideration is its *width*, which should be as great as the barrel will fairly admit, reaching from the bottom of the barrel to the groove *barely*, excepting when the barrel cover is hollowed out, when it may reach it fully. If the spring is not wide enough its working will be irregular ; if too wide then it will bind in the barrel. The next point is the thickness, and it is most important that this should be correct for the watch to perform satisfactorily. If the spring is too thick the action of the escapement will be hurried, and its rate unsteady, and the chain more liable to break ; while, if too thin, the escapement will be sluggish, and the watch apt to stop altogether. The *strength* of the spring should be such that, when of the proper length, hooked in the barrel and wound

up, it may cause the barrel to make about three-quarters of a
turn more than is required by the length of a chain that
occupies the fusee when fully wound. The *length* of a spring
should be such that when wound in the barrel it should occupy
about one-third of its diameter. Having gauged the width
and found the corresponding springs, one of the proper
strength will be found as a rule to be one that is a little larger
in diameter than the barrel, or one that would almost fill the
barrel if it were wound in, so that it is necessary to break off a
short piece that the barrel may not be too full. This applies
to the springs as bought from the makers, coiled within a wire
ring, and is merely given as an approximate guide to selection.
Having selected a spring apparently suitable, it must be
shortened as much as is necessary and hooked in, when it
must be finally tested by holding the barrel tight in the left
hand and winding up the spring by means of a pair of sliding
tongs attached to the squared end of the barrel arbor, and observing how many times it causes the barrel to turn. If it
makes an insufficient number of turns the spring is too thick ,
if too many, then it is too thin. Although this may be stated
as a general rule, it is not without exceptions, as, for example,
in verge watches it is occasionally expedient to use a somewhat weaker spring than will only make the proper number of
turns, owing to an imperfect and unequal balance-wheel not
admitting of a close and correct escapement. There are two
methods of hooking in mainsprings : in one the hook is in the
barrel, and the spring only requires a hole in it near the end ;
in the other the hook is attached to the spring, a hole being
formed in the barrel to receive it. In replacing a spring which
only requires a hole in the end, it must be carefully tempered
by means of a *small* flame so applied that the spring may be
gradually and equally tempered from the end where the hole is
to be, which should be rather soft, to about half an inch of its

length. The hole should be square, as being the least liable to constrain the spring, and prevent its proper action in the barrel. It is usual, after making the hole, which is punched with a pair of mainspring-nippers, to pass a file lightly across the end of the spring and round off the corners, giving it a neat and workmanlike appearance. When the hook is to be attached to the spring, the latter is tempered in the manner already described, and a small round hole punched in it. A piece of hooking-in wire is then fitted to the hole in the barrel and placed in the jaws of a pair of sliding-tongs in such a manner that a pivot may be filed on it to fit the hole in the spring, and cause the piece of hooking-in wire to form a hook standing at the proper angle to suit the hole in the barrel. The hooking-in wire is then put in the vice, and the mainspring firmly secured to it by riveting, when the length of the wire is cut off, leaving only sufficient to form the hook. The end of the spring is usually finished like the other, but left pointed instead of round.   •

The breakage of a spring is always liable to cause other damage, as bent teeth or pivots, or sometimes one of these gets broken, and it is necessary to ascertain whether such damage has been done before setting the watch going again.

To repair the chain.—A very frequent occurrence is the breaking of the chain, and to repair it neatly and strongly only a small amount of application is required. One end of the broken chain must consist of a double, and the other end of a single link. Rest the broken chain upon a piece of hard wood, and with the edge of a sharp penknife slightly raise one end of the outside (double) link nearest the end of the chain, keeping the thumb-nail of the left hand upon it in such a manner that only one rivet is loosened in the link. Turn the chain over and loosen the corresponding end of the opposite link in the same manner. Take the chain in one hand and the short broken link with a pair of pliers in the other, and give a sharp pull, when the piece will easily come out, leaving the free ends of the link ready to receive the inside link of the other part of the chain. Take a piece of steel wire, such as a sewing-needle, tempered to a blue colour, and taper it down with a smooth file until it passes through the holes in the links Place the chain in position upon a piece of soft wood and join up with the pin. Press it in quite tight, then with the nippers cut off as closely as possible and file off the rough projecting ends with a very smooth file until nearly level with the chain. A few taps with a small round-faced hammer will complete the job.

In placing the chain together for riveting, take care that both hooks are towards the same side Though easy to describe, the mending of a chain is by no means easy to do, and it often happens that an experienced hand will break off two or three links before succeeding in getting a satisfactory joint.

To remedy a chain running flat or off the fusee.—If a chain run flat on the barrel, or slip up the fusee when winding, it must be carefully examined, and the cause found out. The chain running flat on the barrel is generally caused by a faulty chain, though sometimes through the barrel being out of upright, and also if the chain is too wide for the spiral in the fusee. The chain should be examined to see that it goes into the groove in the fusee, and that it fills it entirely ; then if the barrel and the axis of the fusee are both upright it is only necessary to stiffen the chain by hammering it along the rivets, and then, unless a very bad one, it will not turn over flat. It may result from the chain being too wide, then the remedy is a new chain. It may be found that the spiral projection on the fusee, which separates each turn of the chain from the next, has become bent or broken in places, so that the safe guidance of the chain cannot be reliedon. If the damage be serious, the fusee should be recut; but if trifling, it may be rectified by carefully restoring the injured part as nearly as possible to its proper position. When the chain runs off without any apparent cause it may frequently be remedied by changing it end for end, or by taking a very little off from the edge of the chain along its entire length.

To tighten a barrel cover —When a barrel cover is loose, it should be covered with a piece of thin paper and gently tapped with a round-faced hammer all round the edge. If carefully done this operation will spread the cover a little, without marking it.

To put in a new barrel arbor.—There are three kinds of arbors commonly in use—the plain English arbor, the plain Geneva arbor, and the Geneva arbor with solid ratchet. The fitting of an arbor of either kind requires to be done very carefully, it being absolutely necessary that the pivots should be accurately fitted, and the endshakes very exact, for the barel to run true and give satisfaction. Either of the plain arbors can be made from a piece of ordinary round steel; or an arbor may be obtained in the rough from the tool shops. In the former case it will be desirable to turn the steel somewhat nearly to shape on a foot-lathe; but when bought in the rough the arbor is quite ready for the more exact turning which is better done on the turns

A screw ferrule is attached to one end of the arbor, and the body or centre part is first turned to the proper width and diameter, the measurement being taken from the old arbor by means of the pinion-gauge. The arbor is then turned down and polished until it fits the holes in the barrel just tight, when a round broach passed lightly into the holes will give the necessary freedom. If an English arbor, the next step will be to turn the top pivot and fit it into the name-plate, and afterwards file the square on the other end of the arbor to receive the ratchet. If a Geneva arbor, the square must be made for the finger-piece of the stopwork and the lower pivot finished before the top or winding square, which also receives the ratchet.

In filing these squares, great care must be taken to make them really square. The best plan to ensure success is to turn a line where the square is to end, and file them up in the turns between the centres. The ends of the squares and pivots are usually finished in the screw-head tool. A hole is drilled obliquely into the body of the arbor to receive the mainspring hook, which is made by driving in very tight a piece of tempered steel, which is afterwards filed to shape.

In case of a Geneva arbor with solid ratchet, it is necessary to obtain the arbor in the rough, and advisable to have that kind which are half finished, for the body is then screwed on and the ratchet polished. It is not easy to tap a good thread suitable for this purpose with the ordinary screw-plates ; and if an arbor must be used, not already screwed by the proper plates, it will be found much better to accurately fit on the body with a plain round hole, and secure it with a steel pin. This kind is generally found where the barrel arbor has the bottom pivot unsupported, and anyone unaccustomed to fine turning is not likely to make a good job of fitting a new one.

To put in a new barrel.—When a new barrel becomes necessary, as it sometimes does, either from the barrel cracking across where the hook is, or from having been spoilt by unskilful treatment, the best plan is to send the old barrel to the material dealers, and obtain a new one of the same size. The new barrel will require to be fitted to the arbor, and a little finishing, and it is much better and cheaper than attempting to make one.

Bent teeth are straightened by means of the screwdriver used as a lever against the root of the adjacent teeth, and bent pivots may be held in the jaws of the pliers and the pinion bent with the fingers in the direction and to the extent required. For such a purpose pliers, having the jaws lined with brass are used, so that the pivot is not bruised, and the bending has to be done with great care.

Broken pivots may be replaced by drilling up the old pinion, which may possibly require softening for the purpose, and putting a plug of steel in, which is then made into a pivot. To centre the broken pinion correctly, the watchmaker proceeds thus: first the end is made tolerably flat with Arkansas stone, the pinion is then mounted in the turns with a screw ferrule on it, and the broken end resting in a groove cut across the T rest; the point of the graver is brought against the end, and the work turned with a drill-bow, its circumference always bearing in the groove, whilst the graver rests on the T, and with its point centres the pinion-end.

A broken verge must be replaced by a new one, and this is a job requiring great skill and practice. A pair of turns having suitable centres—that is to say, very fine female ones—are wanted; also a small screw ferrule to fix on the verge, and a small whalebone drill-bow with a horsehair in place of gut. A small graver will also be required to do the actual turning, and a proper tool, called a " Jacot," is almost essential on which to polish and finish off the pivots. The first thing is to select a suitable verge. It should be of such a length that, when the wheel is kept up close against the brass, the bottom pallet reaches beyond the wheel just sufficiently to allow of perfect freedom of the brass when pivoted in, without fear of the bottom pallet rubbing the potence, or the seat of the balance being too high. Having found a suitable verge, secure a light screw ferrule upon it near the brass, so that the top pallet is within the ferrule, mount it on the turns, and see that the verge itself runs perfectly true. If bent, it must either be straightened or replaced by another. With a pinion-gauge take the size of the brass for the balance-spring collet to fit on tight, and proceed to turn down the brass of the new verge till the gauge passes. Re-set the pinion-gauge to the size of the hole in the balance, and turn off as much as may be necessary for the seat of the balance, taking care to fit it on very tight and not too low. With the graver remove the brass that comes through the balance, leaving only just sufficient to make a firm rivet when the balance is finally put on in its proper place. Turn the bottom pivot perfectly true with the shoulder close up to the bottom pallet, slightly reduce the size of the turned pivot with a smooth pivot file, and fit it in its hole, then burnish and round up the pivot. It is advisable now to put the balance on its seat, and stand the verge in its place, to see if the balance is the correct height, as it may be easily let on a little further if necessary before turning the top pivot. If the height is correct, turn the top pivot true, then file and burnish till it goes in its hole ; finally, shorten till the endshake is correct, and round up the end quite smooth. Rivet on the balance so that the bankings are correct, and reduce the pallets to the necessary width and polish the faces and you have finished, with the exception of putting on the balance-spring.

GLOSSARY

*Of Terms, Tools, Materials, Parts and Processes used
in Watchwork.*

Adjusting Rod.—This is employed to test the force of
the main-spring as conveyed to the fusee, in watches that are
furnished with this latter adjunct. The usual form of adjusting-rod is a steel rod about a foot long and about one-tenth of
an inch diameter. Near one of its ends it has a pair of jaws
capable of clipping the fusee arbor, or wind up square, at right
angles to the length of the rod. A couple of weights slide
along the rod, and may be fixed at any desired place by set-
screws having milled heads. In use the adjusting-rod is fixed
to the fusee arbor, the movement is held up edgeways, and the
power of the spring on the fusee arbor is gauged by sliding
the weights along the rod till it is balanced. The chain is
wound on the fusee gradually by turning the movement round,
and the power of the spring tested continually by the weighted
rod. By this means it is easy to see if the varied power of
the spring exercises a constant unvarying force on the arbor of
the great wheel. That is to say, whether the snail of the fusee
accurately compensates the constantly varying power of the
spring, and thus ensures a uniform impelling force to the
escapement.

Alarm Watch.—A watch which is provided with the
additional mechanism necessary for sounding an alarm. The
instrument is so arranged that it may be set to sound the
alarm after a specific interval of time. Alarm clocks and timepieces are very commonly used, but watches adapted for the

same purpose are seldom seen, except in the possession of collectors of curiosities.

Anchor Escapement.— Lever escapements are often so called, the term being particularly applicable to those in which the pallet arms take a form representing that of a ship's anchor. Foreign watches with the ordinary lever escapement are usually called anchors. The first escapement of this kind appears to have been made about 1680, by Clement, though the merit of the invention is claimed for Hooke. In the early forms the recoil was on both pallets; they are now made with one pallet dead beat, and termed half dead beat or half recoil. Used in clockwork.

Anvil.—In watchwork plain blocks serve all ordinary

Fig. 1. ANVIL TO HOLD IN BENCH-VICE.

Fig. 2. ANVIL MOUNTED ON BLOCK.

purposes in anvil work. The small stake on the claw of the bench-vice is sufficient for most purposes. Some peculiar occasions occur when the beck-iron of an anvil is useful, and diminutive counterparts of the ordinary blacksmith's anvil are made for use in watchwork.

Arbors.—These are tapering mandrels of steel, to which are fitted ferrules, so that they may be rotated with a drill bow. Arbors are used on the turns for the purpose of turning collets, rings and wheels, and any other objects that are most conveniently mounted on a mandrel. Arbors are comprised in sets, the range being generally in accordance with the number.

A set usually consists of from twenty to forty tapering steel spindles, each fitted with a ferrule, and graduating in size from about five-thirty-seconds of an inch in diameter and two inches long to most minute dimensions. The largest size employed

Fig 3. PLAIN ARBOR   Fig. 4. SPLIT ARBOR.

in watchwork is about one-eighth of an inch in diameter and an inch and three-quarters long. Each arbor is pointed at both ends, and slightly tapering. Those axes in a watch which are not pinions are called arbors—*e.g*, the fusee arbor

Archimedian Drill Stock.—These drill stocks are actuated by a nut, which, by being worked along a very quick-threaded screw, causes it to revolve. The stock usually is made of twisted pinion wire, or square steel twisted into a

FIG. 5. ARCHIMEDIAN DRILL-STOCK.

screw-like form. The nut is held in the left hand and worked up and down the stock. One end of the stock is provided with a disc, free to revolve, and forming a means of applying pressure to the drill which is fitted in the other end.

Balance.—The wheel that controls the rate of the watch, moving with a vibrating motion caused by the action of the escapement and that of the balance-spring, the first driving the wheel from its point of rest and the latter causing the recoil. The length of the vibration of a balance is increased or diminished, to make the watch go slower or faster, by letting out or taking up the balance-spring. Ordinary balances are made of a low quality of gold or of brass, but compensation balances (which see), or imitations of them, are now of more frequent occurrence. Steel is an unsatisfactory metal to employ in making balances, as it is liable to become magnetised. A balance should be perfectly true and in one plane, the weight to be as much as possible at the circumference; the form should be one which offers least resistance to the air, and the material should be that which, if in other respects suitable, contains the greatest weight in the least volume. Balances are now invariably annular, but originally they were in the form of a rod, with balance weights at each end, and from this the name was probably derived.

Balance Poising-Tool.—This is a contrivance for supporting the balance staff by its pivots so that the poise of the

Fig 6 BALANCE POISING-TOOL. Fig 7. BALANCE POISING-TOOL.

balance may be noticed. There are many forms in which this tool is made. Its essentials are two parallel knife edges, usually made adjustable as to their distance apart—having notches in which the pivots rest. Any balance thus supported by its axis will, if it is not perfectly in equipoise, at once show a disposition to rest with one particular part downwards.

Balance-Spring.—In pocket watches, where a balance is the controlling regulator, a spring is used to effect on the balance what gravity effects on the pendulum of a clock; this spring is always tending to pull the balance to its point of rest, but when once set in vibration the inertia of the balance, at each vibration, takes it over the point of rest, and the power of the mainspring being felt through the impulse of the escapement causes the balance to perform a longer arc of vibration. There are several terms in general use synonymous to balance spring, as hair-spring, pendulum-spring, spiral-spring, &c. Watches were first made without any balance-spring, the invention being accredited to Hooke, in the middle of the seventeenth century, and after its application to watches the accuracy of their timekeeping was so much improved that a minute-hand was added to the hour-hand, which up to then had been the most minute division attempted in pocket timekeepers.

A balance-spring may require to be made weaker; this is effected by grinding the spring thinner. Remove the spring from the collet and place it upon a piece of peg-wood cut to fit the centre coil. A piece of soft iron wire, flattened so as to pass freely between the coils, and charged with a little pulverized oil-stone and oil, will serve as a grinder, and with it the strength of the spring may soon be reduced. Operations will be confined to the centre coil, for no other part of the spring will rest sufficiently against the wood to enable it to be ground, but this will generally suffice. The effect will be rather rapid, therefore be careful, or the spring may be made too weak before expected.

Balance-Staff.—The axis of the balance, usually exclusively applied to the lever escapement. In the event of a broken staff a new one may be made as follows :—

In the first place the old balance-staff should serve as a model, unless it has any radical defects. The balance is knocked off the brass collar on the old staff and a rough staff selected of approximate dimensions. These staffs are sold in the rough by all watch material dealers, but one may be made by driving a steel arbor into a collet of hard brass. The steel should be hardened and tempered just sufficient to allow it to be turned with the graver. A screw ferrule is fixed to the staff and it is mounted in the turns, the length is reduced to a trifle over the finishing size, paying due attention to the relative length of the staff that projects both above and below the brass. The brass is then turned to fit the balance and the balance-spring collet, and the length is made right. The staff itself is then turned down to fit the hole in the roller. The pivots are then made, gauging the position at the shoulders by means of the pinion gauge, using the old staff to measure by. The diameter is got by trying in the jewel holes. The body of the staff is polished, as are the pivots, with redstuff on a bell-metal burnisher, English workmen generally using the turnbench with specially made centres, but the Jacot tool is far more convenient. When the staff is finished the balance is riveted on true, and should be at the precise height, so that it will not be necessary to use a punch to raise or lower it. Very careful handling and constant gauging are the principal requisites for making a balance-staff; failing the former the partly-finished staff is likely to be broken, and by not paying sufficient heed to the latter some part will be made too small.

Banking Pins.—These are pins put in various escapements to prevent them from overbanking, that is, the pallets from getting beyond the range of the escapement's action.

Bar.—Another name for bridge, which see.

Barrel.—The hollow cylindrical case which contains the mainspring. Also called box. When the periphery has teeth on it driving the train, it is said to be a going barrel; foreign watches invariably have going barrels, which economise space and cost by dispensing with the fusee, chain, &c. One end of the barrel, called the cover, or lid, is movable, being fitted to snap in its place.

Beat.—The tick or sound produced by the action of the escapement; when isochronous, the watch is said to be in beat.   Watches usually beat about sixteen or eighteen thousand times each hour.

In all watch escapements the arbor that carries the balance, whether it is called a verge, a cylinder, or a staff, has to be placed in a certain arbitrary position relatively to the next piece which moves it, in order to ensure the correct action of the escapement.   When it occupies this position it is said to be in beat; when otherwise, out of beat.   This position is necessarily determined by the connection of the balance-spring with the plate, and one of the functions of the balance-spring is to continually restore the balance, and with it the arbor, to its neutral position.   The operation of finding the exact place for the balance-spring to be secured in the stud by means of a pin is called setting the watch in beat.   An explanation of the practical method of setting the verge watch in beat will, to a great extent, apply generally.

Put the end of the balance-spring through the stud so as to bring the verge approximately to its correct position, and pin it moderately tight, taking the precaution to have the spring within the curb pins and quite flat, then put on the cock.   Hold the movement in the left hand, and, with the thumb of the right hand, slowly and carefully press forward the contrate wheel, allowing each escape of a tooth to be quite distinct, and observe how much the balance is drawn to the right in order to allow the escape to take place, and how much to be left.   If it is found that the distances are equal the watch is in beat; if unequal, the cock must be removed, the pin withdrawn a little, and the balance-spring moved in the direction necessary to make the distances equal.   When this is correct the pin must be pressed in tight, the balance spring set quite flat, working equally between the curb pins, and finally the cock screwed on firmly.

Bench Keys.—Double-ended keys for winding watches.

Bench Vice.—As watchwork is only light work, a small vice is all that a watchmaker requires. The tool fixes to the bench by a clamp screw. The jaws are usually about two inches wide. In the left-hand ends of the jaws there are always several indentations; these are for taking the pointed end of the bow drill when drilling. The top of the claw is generally provided with a small surface for stake riveting and flattening drills, &c. Bench vices frequently have jaws opening parallel, and are fitted with small anvils; some swivel round to any angle, and in many details are elaborated.

Fig. 8. BENCH-VICE.

Blowpipe.—The ordinary blowpipe is a tapering tube about eight inches long and one-third of an inch diameter at the largest end. The small end is perforated with a pin hole. The uses of the blowpipe are various, but it is principally used in hardening and tempering, and in soldering.

Boiling Pan.—A small copper pan, very like the domestic frying pan but somewhat deeper, comparatively, used for boiling parts of watches that have been treated with shellac or similar material. By boiling the part in methylated spirit the shellac is dissolved.

Bolt.—The piece by which a movement is held in the case, usually made of steel, fixed to the pillar-plate, and catching in the rim of the case; a spring, called the bolt-spring, forcing the bolt forward, it being held by a screw, and movable radially with the plate by having a slot through which the screw passes.

Bow Pliers.—Used for opening the bow of a watch so that it may be placed on the pendant.   It will be seen by the

Fig. 9. BOW PLIERS.

illustration that these pliers have a joint contrived to allow the jaws to open when the handles are compressed.

Bows.—Generally called drill bows.   They are elastic rods having a cord by which a reciprocating rotary motion is given to drills and work mounted for turning.   Whalebone and cane are the most usual materials for bows used for watchwork. They taper from the butt to the point, which usually has a hook.   The largest are about fifteen inches long, and about three-eighths diameter at the largest part.   Small bows are from four to six inches long and very slight.   These are strung with a single horse-hair; the large bows have cat-gut for cords. Bows were used for driving lathes long before the application of fly wheels.   The bow of a watch is the ring affixed to the pendant to form a means of attaching the watch to a guard; the long steel screw by which the bow is secured is called the bow-screw.

Bow Saw.—The usual saw employed in watchwork is an

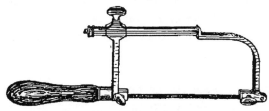

Fig. 10. BOW SAW.

adjustable bow saw or frame saw, which takes the saw blades

used for piercing metal and for fretwork. Saw blades, of much greater width, mounted in a rigid bow frame, and miniature back saws are also used. The saw blade should always be

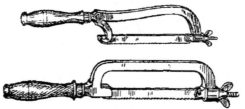

Figs. 11, 12. Bow Saws.

mounted in its frame to cut when pulled, not when being pushed away, that is to say, the teeth should slant towards the handle.

Brass Edge.—A circular plate of brass on which the dial is pinned by its three feet; the brass edge being itself pinned to the pillar plate, the joint by which the movement is held in the case being fixed indifferently to the plate or brass edge by rivets or a screw. The brass edge lifts the dial from the plate to allow space for the motion wheels, and is unnecessary, and not used in movements having solid pillar plates; that is, those having a raised rim, for the dial to rest on, solid with the plate.

Breguet Spring.—A balance-spring having the outer coil bent up out of the plane of the spiral, and towards the centre of the balance staff near which it is fixed, so that, during the vibrations of the balance, the coiling and uncoiling of a Breguet spring is more concentric than an ordinary one. The spring is named from its inventor, and is often found in high-class watches.

Bridge.—A piece resting on the plate at both ends, and secured by two screws, the central part being cut away to allow of one or more bearings for pivots. Bridges are only found in movements of the skeleton class, and are the barrel bridge and centre wheel bridge, bar being a synonymous term. When resting on, and secured at one place only, it is called a cock.

Bright Grey.—A process of finishing brass, affected by means of rotten-stone mixed with oil and applied with a box-wood slip. The surface of the work is first prepared by greying with water-of-ayr stone

Broach.—A tool used for enlarging holes. It is usually made of a five-sided conical prism of steel, the angles of which form the cutting edges. Very small ones, called pivot broaches, are used for reaming out the holes for pivots. Plain cylindrical broaches are used to polish the holes finally. These are called burnishing broaches, and by compressing the metal they harden that around the hole.

Brushes.—Watchmakers' brushes are in constant requisition but are seldom kept in proper order. A soft brush for rough work is useless, a hard one for fine work is ruinous, and a dirty brush of any kind is a nuisance. Some brushes are cleaned with dry bread; some by laying a piece of tissue or other paper across the wide-open jaws of the bench vice, the sharp corners formed by the jaws taking off on the paper a little of the dirt. These methods are imperfect. A good way to clean a brush is with soap and water—warm water being preferable. Wet two brushes, soap them, and then rub them together in plenty of water till perfectly clean. An objection to this method is the delay in drying. Much injury is done to the appearance of the movement by injudicious brushing, and the watch grows prematurely old in looks by such treatment.

Buff Sticks.—Slips of wood, covered with buff leather, and used in numerous polishing processes, some abrasive material being spread on them suited to the work in hand.

Bumping-up Stake.—A steel stake, either round, square, or triangular, at one end and hollow at the other; the solid end being used for hammering work on, and the hollow end for resting wheels and balances on when the arms require slightly bending by a gentle tap with the hammer.

Fig. 13.
BUMPING-UP STAKE.

Burnishers.—Tools used for burnishing generally, but a name more particularly applied to highly polished pieces of steel used on the surface of pivots, and which impart to these an equivalent lustre. Burnishers must be kept scrupulously clean and bright to produce satisfactory results. Sticks of alloys of tin, gun-metal, and other materials used for applying polish, are by some called burnishers, though polishers is a more correct designation. The plain, round brooches used for burnishing holes are also called burnishers. They are particularly good tools to use in opening pivot holes, as they compress the metal and so make a harder bearing.

Burnt Bone.—A material used for cleaning brushes and considered preferable to chalk as being less gritty and dusty. Burnt bone is not sold commonly, but it may be easily prepared by placing ox bones in a crucible and allowing them to remain for some hours in a brisk fire. The crucible should remain in the fire till it has died out; when the burned bones are cold, soft white pieces may be selected for rubbing the brush upon, and so cleaning it.

Bush.—A piece of hard metal inserted in the plate or cock of a watch to form a bearing for a pivot. The bushes usually employed are made in quantities on the Continent, and sold at a small price. They are made of hard brass wire, in lengths of about half an inch, and each end is drilled up, and the outside turned truly concentric with the boring, a nick being cut to facilitate breaking off the bush when it is pressed into a hole broached out specially to receive it. These bushes are best known by their continental name, *bouchons ;* they are made in graduated sizes to suit the various dimensions of the pivots in the different parts of the train, and for large and small movements. The smaller pivots, however, generally are fitted to jewel holes.

Calendar Watch.—The mechanism of this description of watch is so far increased that not only are the minutes and hours indicated, but additional hands or dials show the days, the weeks, and the months—sometimes the year, also with the phases of the moon, &c. The most simple mechanism merely records the lapse of every twenty-four hours, the mechanism being shifted automatically one day forward at about midnight, and the dial showing the date of the month has to be set right at the commencement of each month. In perpetual calendars the entire records of the days, months, and years are kept automatically ; the long and short months—*i.e.,* those with few and many days—are provided for in the mechanism, which extends so far that the extra day in February of Leap Year is duly indicated on the calendar, this involving the use of a wheel which revolves only once during four years.

Callipers.—A tool shaped like a figure **8**, made of brass,

Fig. 14 PLAIN CALLIPERS.   Fig. 15. GAUGE CALLIPERS.

and jointed in the middle. It is used for testing the truth of wheels on their axes. A wheel to be tested is put between the jaws, which have small indentations to receive the pivot ends. The wheel is spun round with the fingers, and a straight edge held near its periphery. When the wheel is perfectly at right angles to its axis it is said to be "in flat," and when perfectly concentric it is "in round." When both in flat and in round an object is said to be "true."

Cannon Pinion.—The steel hollow pinion which fits on the centre-wheel arbor, and on which the minute-hand is generally fixed; on the cannon-pinion the hour wheel revolves, and in it the centre arbor fits, spring tight, to allow of the hands being shifted, by turning the cannon, without moving the arbor. Where the hands are set from the front, the top of the cannon is made square to take a key; in those watches set from the back, the centre pinion is hollow and the cannon carried by a set-hands-square, passing through from the back usually, though sometimes solid with the cannon-pinion, and fitted with a square at the back.

Cap.—A brass case made to fit over the entire movement, and so protect it from dust, &c. Usually the cap is a round hollow box, which precisely fits the movement, the edge resting on the pillar-plate, and the balance-cock sometimes coming through the cap; it is commonly met with in old verge watches, and in full-plate English levers, but is now seldom made.

Case Stake.—A kind of anvil used for resting watch cases upon when hammering them to take out bruises, &c. The stake is usually a mushroom-shaped piece of steel, having the top highly polished. Case stakes made of boxwood are also used.

Case-Winding Watch.—Watches which are contrived to be wound by means of the case are so called. In some, the action of opening and shutting the case winds up the movement. Others have the rim or bottom of the case connected with the winding arbor, so that it may be actuated by revolving or oscillating one of these. This form of winding mechanism is but seldom employed, and has no practical value.

Centre Seconds.—In these watches the train is so arranged that the fourth wheel carrying the seconds-hand is in the centre of the dial. Stop-watches usually have centre seconds, and in some cases independent centre seconds. This latter is a movement consisting of two distinct trains, so that when the seconds-hand, which is driven independently by one train, is stopped, the other hands continue to go on, and, in fact, the watch indicates the time continuously, whether the independent train is stopped or going. The motion wheels in centre seconds movements are generally placed in the usual position, a stud being fixed in the centre having a hole through its centre to allow the seconds pivot to pass; the cannon-pinion is enlarged sufficiently to pass over the stud, the other wheels being as usual. The motion is usually imparted from a duplicate of the cannon-pinion on the set-hands-square of the centre-pinion gearing into the minute-wheel.

Centre Wheel.—That wheel of the train which is the centre of the handwork, usually the one on the axis driven by the great wheel, and in the centre of the plate, its arbor carrying the minute-hand. Though displaced by the exigencies of peculiarities, as in the centre seconds watch, still the wheel retains its name. In some movements, as those which are constructed to go for a week, the centre wheel is not driven direct from the great wheel, but through the intervention of an extra wheel and pinion.

Centres.—There are many variously formed centres fitted to the turns. Round steel wire, which fits the turns, and having the ends made of a form to suit the work, are the most general. Brass centres are also used. Nearly all watchwork is turned between female centres, but occasionally points are employed.

Centring Tool.—A tool for centring work to be mounted for turning. It usually consists of a cone, in the centre of which a cutting point protrudes. Work to be centred is revolved in the cone, and the cutting point marks the centre.

A method of centring small rod metal for turning is by means of a tool made by grinding the end of a small round file in three facets to produce a cutting point, and to locate the centre by the eye alone.

Fig. 16.
CENTRING TOOL.

Chain.—Used to communicate the power of the mainspring to the fusee. These chains have flat links strung together with rivets, each of which passes through three links, these running alternately in pairs and singly; the links are punched out of flat steel and are of very small size. Steel wire is used for the rivets. At each end of the chain a hook is put, one to catch in a hole in the barrel, the other to hook over a pin in the fusee. Chains for pocket watches vary in size considerably, but the average length is about six inches, and contains about six hundred pieces, consisting of the links, the rivets, and the two hooks, the whole weighing perhaps less than two grains. Chains are only used in conjunction with fusees. The method of putting the chain on a fusee is this :— Get the barrel and fusee in such positions that the holes for the chain hooks are towards the outside edge of the movement; then put the ratchet-wheel on the barrel and pass the chain through from the fusee side, under the pillar, and put the hook in the hole in the barrel. Now wind the barrel round, keeping the chain tight the while with the fingers, and when all is wound on the barrel let the click fall in the ratchet, and hook the other end of the chain in the fusee. There should be just

F

sufficient tension on the chain to prevent its slipping off, and you can now regulate the coils on the periphery of the barrel so that the chain will lead properly on to the groove cut in the fusee. Then set up the spring by giving the barrel arbor half a turn : this gives the necessary tension to afford the power required to make the watch go. Now wind the watch in the usual way, carefully guiding the chain, if requisite, so that it passes into the groove in the fusee, and the job is done. Setting up a spring is a process which should not be done by an inexperienced person who does not understand the *rationale* of it.

Chain Guard.— The piece forming a stop to prevent overwinding. Described under the heading of stopfinger.

Chalk.—The material used in watch-work is usually prepared chalk. The chalk is thoroughly pulverised and mixed with clear rain-water in the proportion of two pounds to the gallon. Stir well and let it stand about two minutes. In this time the gritty matter will have settled to the bottom. Pour the water into another vessel, slowly, so as not to stir up the settlings. Let stand until entirely settled, and then pour off as before. The settlings in the second vessel will be your prepared chalk, ready for use as soon as dried. Spanish whiting treated in the same way makes a very good cleaning or polishing powder. Some add a little jeweller's rouge, which gives the powder a colour, and adds to its value in the eyes of the uninitiated. In cases where a sharper polishing powder is required, it may be prepared in the same way from rotten-stone. Chalk is frequently manufactured specially by adding a solution of carbonate of soda to a solution of chloride of calcium (both cheap salts) so long as a precipitate is thrown down. The solutions should be carefully filtered through paper before being mixed, and dust should be rigorously excluded. The white powder which falls down is carbonate of lime, or chalk, and when carefully washed and dried it forms a most excellent polishing powder for the softer metals The particles are almost impalpable, but seem to be crystalline, for they polish quickly and smoothly, though they seem to wear away the material so little that its form or sharpness is not injured to any perceptible degree.

Chalk Box.—This is a little box for holding a lump of chalk, upon which to rub the brushes used in cleaning, to free them from grease and dirt. It may be made by nailing up a small box from three inches to four inches square underneath the work-board, with a small piece of wood to prevent the chalk from falling out in front; or by fixing a piece of wood from the right-hand support to a place underneath the work-board, when the chalk will wedge itself sufficiently firm for the purpose.

Chamfers.—These are tools used for making hollows in watch plates, &c., such as the shallow indents for oil around pivot holes. The best form of chamfer for this purpose is a steel wheel mounted in a notch, cut diameter ways, in the end of a properly made shaft. The wheel projects slightly, and when the tool is rotated with a reciprocating motion the wheel cuts a hollow of circular section, the radius corresponding to the size of the wheel. For cutting, the edge of the wheel is left quite square, but when rounded it serves as a burnisher. Two wheels of the same diameter, one to cut and one to burnish, are usually mounted in the opposite ends of one shaft. Different diameters produce different sized chamfers, wheels from one-tenth of an inch to a quarter of an inch diameter being commonly used.

Chronograph.—This form of watch registers on the dial, by means of dots, the time at which a certain action takes place, as the pressing of a button or push-piece. In the usual form of chronograph there is a centre seconds with one hand precisely over the other; the lower hand has at its point a receptacle for ink, and the upper hand is bent at right angles towards the dial and passes through the ink. On pressing a button the top hand is depressed, and touching the dial leaves on it an ink spot, the hand immediately rising again, so that the going of the watch is not impeded. Chronographs sometimes take the place of split-seconds, but they are not generally used.

Chronometer.—Strictly a measurer of time, and equally applicable to the primitive contrivances used for that purpose as to the finely adjusted instruments which the highest skill of modern horologists can produce. The term is, however, generally applied more particularly to the chronometer escapement, originated by Berthoud, and applied by Harrison in the second quarter of the eighteenth century. The latter received a Government award of £20,000 for perfecting a chronometer which was tested on one of the king's ships in 1758. Arnold made improvements, and Earnshaw brought the chronometer to its present state of perfection. The balance of the chronometer is always compensated, and, from the fact of the impulse being communicated only once to each complete to and fro vibration of the balance, this form of escapement is not suited to the jars and shocks incidental to pocket wear, hence it is chiefly confined to ships' chronometers.

Chucks.—These are appliances for holding work whilst being operated upon by the tool. Usually the term is restricted

Fig. 17. ARBOR CHUCK.

to pieces attached to the lathe-mandrel, several of which are shown below.

Fig. 17 shows an arbor chuck for holding saws, laps, &c.,

which are fixed by the nut on the end. Fig. 18 shows a similar chuck, but longer and having a milled nut. Fig. 19 shows a

Fig. 18. ARBOR CHUCK.

chuck constructed like the wire chuck, but bored out tapering so as to hold tapering laps, centres, &c., as shown. Fig. 22 is a

Fig. 19. HOLLOW-CONE CHUCK. Fig. 20. LAP TO FIT CONE CHUCK. Fig. 21. CONE-POINT TO FIT CONE CHUCK.

screw chuck, having a thread cut in the outer end with which

Fig. 22. SCREW CHUCK. Fig. 23. LAP TO FIT SCREW CHUCK.

laps and many other small pieces can be screwed for turning. Fig. 24. Face-plate chuck, used to drive work turned between centres and having a dog, such as the one shown at Fig. 43 fixed to it.

The four accompanying illustrations show various forms of cement chucks. Figs. 26 and 27 screw into such chucks as Fig. 30, and Figs. 27 and 28 are used on an arbor chuck. The faces of these chucks

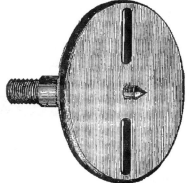

Fig. 24. FACE PLATE.

are covered with cement in which any article may be imbedded and so fixed.

Figs. 25, 26, 27, 28. CEMENT CHUCKS.

Fig. 29 is a sectional view of a shoulder chuck. This is

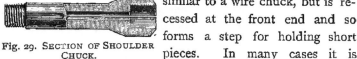

similar to a wire chuck, but is recessed at the front end and so forms a step for holding short

Fig. 29. SECTION OF SHOULDER CHUCK.

pieces. In many cases it is undesirable to have steps cut in wire chucks and the stepping appliance shown on page 130 may be used instead. It has the advantage of being adjustable to any depth.

Fig. 30 shows a tapermouth screw chuck intended to receive small chucks and appliances such as the cement

Fig. 30. TAPER-MOUTH SCREW CHUCK.

chucks, Figs. 25 and 26.

Wire chucks, also called spring chucks and split chucks, are extensively used for holding wire; several illustrations show these chucks.

They are made in a range of sizes which have a uniform difference of $\frac{4}{1000}$ of an inch between each successive size

The smallest size in common use takes wire $\frac{12}{1000}$ inches in diameter, and the largest takes $\frac{200}{1000}$. These chucks are all known by certain numbers according to their size; the numbers

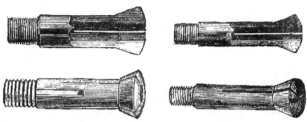

Figs. 31, 32, 33, 34. Wire Chucks. Full size Sections and Perspective Illustrations.

represent an equivalent to tenths of a millimeter; thus number 3 takes $\frac{3}{10}$ of a millimeter, and so on. The construction of split chucks may be seen by the illustrations. There are three radial slots and the coned part jambs in the end of the mandrel, thus firmly gripping the wire perfectly true.

Step chucks are shown at Figs. 35 and 36. These chucks are split, and have steps turned in them, in which discs, or wheels, may be held. The chucks are made of brass, and a set of five

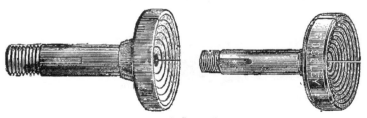

Figs. 35, 36. Step Chucks.

hold all sizes from 5 mm. to 22·5 mm. The steps are sometimes turned specially for any piece which they do not exactly fit, but with a properly graduated set this should not be necessary.

Fig. 37 shows a universal face-plate or chuck, which may be screwed into the mandrel and used in the same way as Fig. 73. The pump centre rod shown at Fig. 38, which is actuated by

Fig. 38. PUMP CENTRE.

Fig. 37. UNIVERSAL FACE-PLATE OR CHUCK.

the fingers passes through the stalk of the chuck. The left-hand end screws into the cone-point, and the right-hand end has a knob for taking hold of. The centre can be used either with or without the spring in action.

Clamps.—A tool used in the bench-vice, having the jaws of a form to adapt them for the purpose intended.

Cleaning.—To give the work a good appearance many methods are adopted. Dipping or soaking the parts in benzine or spirits of wine facilitates the removal of greasy dirt. A good soft brush, occasionally cleansed by rubbing on chalk or burnt bone, and tissue paper to hold the parts in so as to prevent contact with the skin, will be found as good a method as any.

Fig. 39. CLAMPS.

Clepsydra.—Probably the earliest form of time measurer; it was used among the Egyptians, Chaldeans, Greeks and Romans. It is simply an instrument, or vessel, which is filled with water, and records the flow of this fluid. Modifications of the clepsydra are now used for the accurate measurement of small intervals of time. A stream of mercury, flowing from a vessel at a known rate, is directed into a receiver during a certain event, and by weighing the accumulation in the receivers the time that has elapsed may be reckoned.

Clicks.—These are the various detents which act on the ratchet wheels, and prevent the backward motion of the winding arbor. In fusees there are two clicks, made from wire drawn specially to the form required, placed at diametrically opposite points. Going-barrel clicks are of two forms ; one, the side click, is a steel spring, which is screwed by one end to the side of the barrel bridge, having its free end shaped into a click fitting the ratchet teeth ; the other form is a short lever held by a screw, and forced up to its work by a circular spring fixed to the top of the bridge Clicks should always be hardened and tempered, excepting those in fusees ; these latter are made from special wire.

Clock-Watch.—A watch with mechanism to strike the time, as does an ordinary striking clock; the clock-watch strikes automatically, and is thus distinguished from the repeater, which performs the same function, when urged to do so by winding up the mechanism.

Closing Punches.—These are for closing holes which have become too large. The punch is arranged so that it compresses the metal around the hole.

Cock.—A piece serving the purpose of a bridge, but resting only on one end, and held by one screw, as the balance-cock of all watches. The various cocks are generally distinguished by an adjective, indicating the purpose to which they appertain.

Collet.—Any small ring, or washer, used in watch-work, as the balance-spring collet—a brass ring, fitting the collet of the balance axis, in which the inner end of the spring is pinned.

Collet Arbors.—A modification of the plain arbor, to adapt it specially for turning discs having a central hole. Near that end of the arbor opposite the ferrule is a flange of brass, and beyond this the arbor has a thread cut on it, usually left-handed. A steel cone is fitted on this screw, and a small nut forces this cone towards the flange. Any disc having a hole which the cone will fit may be mounted on the collet arbor, and, on screwing up the nut, the work will be forced against the flange and fixed. The cone keeps the disc true radially, and the flange serves the same office flatways. Collet arbors of various sizes are used. Their principal advantage is in holding collets that are too thin to afford a good hold for an ordinary arbor.

Compensation Balance.—A balance constructed to make isochronal beats, notwithstanding changes of temperature. The ordinary annular balance is subject to two variations on increase of temperature. First, the balance itself is expanded, and its inertia consequently increased ; and, secondly, the balance-spring is made more flexible by heat. The usual compensation-balance is made by uniting a ring of steel to one of brass, the latter metal being the outer, the compound ring being carried by a single diametrical bar, in the centre of which the balance staff is fixed. The ring is cut through at diametrically opposite points near to the cross bar, and near the free ends of the segmental circles some heavy-headed screws are put, tapped radially into the rim of the balance. Then the contraction of the two metals of which the balance rim is composed being different, the arcs become more or less bowed, and practically, when the power of the balance-spring is reduced by heat, the extra expansion of the outer metal (brass) in the rim brings the heavy-headed screws nearer the centre, thereby decreasing the inertia of the entire balance. The action of the spring becoming weakened by the same cause, the vibrations of the balance are made isochronous under all temperatures by the proper adjustment of the relative proportions of the spring and the balance. The compensation-balance, as first introduced, consisted of two strips riveted together with numerous small rivets, but Earnshaw perfected the balance to its present form a hundred years ago. It is curious that some compensation-balances are found in watches where they have been for years, and yet the division of the rim, absolutely necessary for any compensation to take place, had never been effected. The accurate adjustment of the compensation by the relative position of the timing-screws is one enjoining extreme care and long trials, which are seldom bestowed.

Contrate Wheel.—Crown Wheel.—A wheel having its teeth cut at right angles to the periphery; the fourth wheel in a verge movement, which drives the escape-wheel pinion, is a crown wheel, and sometimes termed a contrate wheel. This form of wheel is seldom found except in verge watches and old-fashioned clocks, the depthing being very difficult to arrange properly on so small a scale.

Conversion.—A verge movement which has had a lever escapement fitted to it is called a conversion, or converted lever, though it would apparently be more correct to speak of such a watch as a converted verge. Some verge watches, which have certain intrinsic value to their owners, are converted out of caprice, but it is a practice which seldom gives satisfaction, and is now very seldom carried out.

Cork Arbors.—Arbors made somewhat like the ordinary arbor, but in two, and each half provided with a cork disc. Between the two discs objects may be held for turning. The chief use of cork arbors is to hold watch-glasses on the turns, so that their edges may be slightly reduced.

Counter-shafts.—These are intermediaries between the motive power and the machine in motion. They are usually fixed to the back part of the work-bench and are quite indispensable in working some of the apparatus used on the lathe.

Fig. 40. COUNTER-SHAFT.

Fig. 41. COUNTER-SHAFT.

Figs. 40 and 41 show two slightly different forms of counter shafts.

Countersinking Tool.—This tool is employed for making small countersinks where a pin drill is not available, and when it is undesirable to mount the work on a lathe for treatment. The tool consists of a cannon made of steel, with a foot having its lower surface flat and at right angles to the boring of the cannon, the foot projecting on one side only. This cannon is fixed on the watch-plate by means of a hand vice clamping the foot and the plate. When so fixed, cutters, fitting the bore of the cannon, are brought to bear upon the watch-plate. The cutters are kept in position and upright by means of the cannon, and drills, countersinks for jewels, and various other tools, are used. Numerous attachments are applied to the simple counter-sinking tool, such as a stop to regulate the depth of cut. The cutters are of various forms for different purposes ; they are actuated by a drill bow generally, though sometimes they are rotated by the thumb and finger.

Crossing Files.—These are used for filing the arms and inside rims of wheels, technically called "crossing out." The files are taper and have rounded sides, each of a different curvature, so as to be suitable for circles of different radii.

Curb Pins.—The two pins, in the ordinary index or regulator, which confine the motion of the balance-spring so that it is controlled by the regulator, from the stud in which the spring is fixed by pinning.

Cutting Pliers.—Tools used for cutting wire and similar purposes, more generally called nippers, which see.

Cylinder Escapement.—This form of escapement is also known as the horizontal, so called from the fact of the escape-wheel lying horizontally, in distinction from the verge or vertical escapement. This escapement was invented by Tompion, and perfected by Graham, early in the last century ; it is now almost exclusively employed in foreign watches, and is used instead of the lever from motives of economy ; movements of the flattest kind have cylinder escapements. The axis of the balance is a hollow cylinder, cut away to allow the passage of the escape-wheel teeth. It is adopted in Swiss and French watches, being cheap in construction, and allowing the watch to be made very flat. Though excellent for ordinary pocket watches, the cylinder escapement cannot be said to equal the lever and some others, where greater accuracy is required. The drop of the escapement is the cause of much trouble to watch-jobbers, but the following means will enable them to ascertain how far the drops are equal and correct. The movement being slightly wound up, with a fine wire or strip of paper turn the balance till a tooth falls; now try how much shake the escape-wheel has, and allow the tooth to escape; then try again, and go all round the wheel to see how all the teeth and spaces agree in size. To correct any inequality is certainly a job for an expert hand, and directions will not avail much, unless to an expert. When the tooth contained within the cylinder has no freedom, and rubs at the point and heel, there is no internal drop; when the tooth has escaped, and the cylinder shell rubs on the point of one tooth and the heel of the next, then there is no outside drop. The internal drop is increased by reducing the length of the teeth, the external by increasing the space between the teeth. When the drop is very slight, the watch is very liable to stop through the excessive friction; in the case of unequal drop the rate of a watch cannot be maintained, and occasionally stoppages will occur. This fault is found by dotting the balance with spots of rouge and carefully noting the oscillations, which, if unequal, indicate unequal drops. Though this is the usual cause, the same effect may be the result of some teeth lifting more than others. A noisy drop is caused by badly polished surfaces, and in such a case the heel of the cylinder should be carefully noticed. If the escape-wheel

pivot holes are too large, an immense amount of trouble will
be caused, and, in fact, all the end-shakes and side-shakes of
the cylinder and escapement require most careful adjustment.
An excess of oil will also cause an infinity of errors to arise,
and should be most carefully guarded against. The points of
the escape-wheel teeth may catch in a slight burr, which is
sometimes left at the lips of the cylinder, and of course would
stop the watch. This is remedied by polishing the cylinder
and rounding off the points of the escape-wheel teeth.
The balance-spring should be pinned up to have the escapement in perfect beat. This is done by pinning the stud
on the spring so that it is exactly over a dot marked in the
balance for the purpose of showing the position. Sometimes
the lower corner of the heel of the escape-wheel tooth touches
the inside of the cylinder and stops the watch. But all these
defects may be seen, or rather felt, by careful trial. If there
is any doubt of parts touching where they should not, a spot
of rouge put on will at once mark where it touches.

Cylinder Gauge.—This is used to measure the sizes of a
cylinder, both diametrically and across the half shell. The
tool consists of three strips of steel riveted together, with two
longitudinal spaces, each proportionate to the other, and
tapering. The edge of the steel along one side of each opening is graduated, and when the diameter of the cylinder, as
gauged in the wide slot, is coincident with the dimension of
the half-shell, as shown in the narrow slot, the notch in the
cylinder is known to be cut to the correct depth.

Dead-Beat Escapements. — In escapements of this
class the face of the pallet on which the tooth of the escape-
wheel drops is concentric with its centre of motion, and hence
by the further swing of the balance in the supplementary arc
no recoil is effected on the escape-wheel, and the wheel
remains at rest, or dead, till, on the return motion of the

balance, the impulse plane of the pallet is brought under the point of the tooth, and then the power from the train acts on the escapement.

Depthing Tool.—This is an instrument used to test the depthing or gearing of a wheel and pinion or parts of an escapement. The tool consists of two frames, each somewhat resembling a turn bench, which are jointed together and moved by a fine screw. The centres are perfectly parallel to

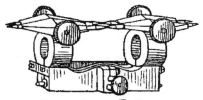

Fig 42 DEPTHING TOOL.

each other, and their distance apart is adjusted by the screw already mentioned. In use the two arbors to be depthed are put between the centres, to run free, but without shake, and the two frames are brought together till the depthing is correct. Pointed ends to the centres afford a means of marking on the watch-plate the correct distance apart for the pivot hole.

Detached Escapement.—This escapement is any one that leaves the balance free of the train excepting at the time when the impulse is given. Chronometer and lever escapements are detached; detached lever is a term not applicable to the rack lever.

Detent.—Very often used to indicate clicks; however, properly speaking, the detent is, that piece of steel which forms a click to the maintaining power. The detent is pivoted into the plates and kept to its place by a steel spring screwed on the pillar-plate and called the detent spring. The detent in a chronometer escapement is that piece which stops the escape-wheel from turning until lifted aside by the roller.

Dial Wheels.—The wheels which lie on the pillar-plate beneath the dial. In ordinary watches these are only the motion wheels (which see), but in complicated mechanism, calendars, &c., the dial wheels are often very numerous.

Dial.—The face of a watch; sometimes made of gold or silver, but more frequently enamelled on copper. Thin sheet copper is punched into form, the holes made and feet soldered on. The surface is then enamelled and baked, the figures and dots for the minutes being painted with a camel-hair brush. An enamel dial made expressly for a movement will have the holes for both hour and seconds hands made sufficiently large by the dial-maker, unless he were instructed to the contrary. Foreign dials may be purchased at tool-dealers' shops, and these have very small holes. The object is probably to allow the holes to be opened sideways to suit the particular movement to which they may be ultimately fitted. It is a tedious operation to enlarge the holes, the best way to do it being with an emery bob, made of shellac and emery, driven with a drill-bow. This will cut the enamel, and the copper is operated upon with a file. Careful treatment is necessary to guard against chipping or cracking the dial Old copper dial-plates are never re-enamelled, but an entirely new dial is made. To those who do not know anything of the process of dial-making, it may not be superfluous to tell how to proceed if a new dial is wanted. Take the watch movement entirely apart; put the pillar-plate and dial-plate, or brass edge in the case, without being pinned together, not even with the joint-pin. Leave the old dial out. Send these portions—the case and plates— to the dial maker with an order for a dial as required, with sunk seconds or otherwise. In the course of a few days the dial will be finished, and you will have to drill small holes through the copper feet for the pins which secure the dial. The hole for the hour-hand socket will probably be large enough, also the hole for the cannon of the seconds-hand. If not, they may be enlarged by the method already mentioned. A dial made specially is far superior to one bought ready made.

Diamantine.—Diamantine consists of crystallised boron, the basis of borax. By melting 100 parts boric acid and 80 parts aluminium, crystals are obtained, the so-called bort, which even attacks diamond. Diamantine bought in commerce is very hard.

Diamond Broaches.—These broaches are made of brass, the size and shape desired. Having oiled them slightly, their surfaces are rolled in fine diamond dust until entirely covered. Place the broach on the face of an anvil, and tap with a light hammer till the grains are imbedded in the brass. Great caution will be necessary in this operation, so as not to flatten the broach. Very light blows are all that will be required; the grains will be driven in much sooner than would be imagined. Some roll the broach between two pieces of smooth steel to imbed the diamond dust. It is a good way, but somewhat more wasteful of the dust. Broaches made on this plan are used for dressing out jewel-holes.

Dog.—Used to grip work for turning between centres.

The dog shown at Fig. 43 is intended for use with the face-plate chuck shown on page 69. The cut is half size, and the work is gripped between the two halves of the dog, the screws serving

Fig 43. DOG.   to draw them together. The tail shown at the upper left-hand corner is placed in the slot of the face-plate.

Double-Bottom Cases.—Those having the "dome" soldered to the "belly," so that the movement cannot be inspected from the back of the case.

Douzieme Gauge.—Spring callipers used for gauging thickness in all parts of watch-work, but especially plates. The douzième is jointed near one end, and has a scale and index on the longer arms. The short arms meet as jaws, and the measurements shown by the index are approximately the twelfth of a line, about seventy-two of these, or six lines, being the limit of range.

Exactly equal measurements are not shown at different openings of the douzième, as the jaws measure a chord whilst the index shows an equally divided arc.

DOUZIEME GAUGE
Fig. 44.

Drills.—The drills used by watchmakers are generally made by filing the cylindrical steel wire slightly tapering, and then spreading the point with a single blow from a tolerably heavy hammer. Using a light hammer and effecting the spreading by a series of gentle taps will effectually spoil the steel. There is not the slightest occasion to anneal the steel for hammering, provided it is moderately soft. For all drills up to one-eighth of an inch diameter the steel should not be forged, as the bulk of the metal is too small to heat to any predetermined temperature with any degree of certainty. Pivot drills can be made from good sewing-needles, which are of convenient form to be readily converted into a drill. Firstly, the needle must be made sufficiently soft for working by heating till it assumes a deep blue colour. The extreme end may be made quite soft, and filed, slightly tapering to a trifle less than the size of the hole to be drilled. The point is now spread out by a sharp blow of a hammer—not by a series of gentle taps, which would cause the metal to crack—and filed up to shape, the point being made more blunt than would be used for drilling ordinary metal. For drilling tempered steel the cutting angles must also be much less than usual. The thickness of the drill across the flattened part should be about a third the diametrical measurement. Finish up the end on a strip of Arkansas stone, a file being too coarse for such small work. It is the great difficulty of getting such a very small piece of steel to an exact predetermined degree of temperature—hot enough to harden, but not so hot that it is burned—which makes the manufacture of these small tools uncertain, and this is abundantly proved by the fact that of half-a-dozen drills made from the same wire, thereby assuring uniformity of quality in the material, it often happens that some are exceedingly good and others of no use whatever, the difference being caused by the manipulation during hardening. This does not apply to drills or other steel things which are of sufficient size to show, by the colour of their surface, how hot they are ; but it is the tiny pieces which, by the contact with the flame, are immediately rendered white-hot that are difficult to manage. By heating the drill and plunging it into the body of a tallow candle the hardening will be effected, but the steel will not be rendered so hard that it crumbles away under pressure in use. Thus, in one operation, the drill will be hardened and tempered. Instead of tallow, white wax, sealing wax, and such like materials are adapted to the purpose. There is another method which finds favour with some : it is to envelope the thin point of the drill in a metal casing, and so get a bulk of metal which can be heated to a nicety, the drill inside being, of course, raised to the same temperature as the surrounding metal ; the whole is then plunged into oil or water. Still there is the difficulty of tempering to overcome, though the danger of burning is avoided ; burnt steel is of no use for tools. The best plan is to exercise the greatest possible care not to over-heat the drill, and harden and temper in one operation by plunging into tallow. The following method dispenses with the hardening process :—Select a round pivot broach ; as sold, they will be found to be tempered to the correct degree of hardness. By means of the split gauge, measure the part of the broach which is the exact diameter required for the intended hole, and break off the steel at that point ; the small piece is used ; it must be broken off if too long, and cemented into a drill-stock by shellac ; an ordinary drill-stock will do, or a piece of brass joint wire serves the purpose. Soft solder may be used instead of shellac ; and if carefully heated the temper will not be drawn. The piece of tapering steel is now formed into a drill by grinding down the sides with a piece of Arkansas stone, and the end shaped up to a cutting angle. The thick end of the broach forms the cutting end, and the ordinary taper of a broach will be quite sufficient to give clearance to the drill, which may be sharpened by grinding until the whole is used.

Drill-stocks.—For the purpose of holding drills when used, such drills being only short pieces without a means of rotating them which the stock furnishes. Ordinary dril-lstocks, for use with the drill bow, are rods of steel with a ferrule near one end, which is pointed. The other end is bored up and a notch cut about half through the diameter to afford a hold for the drills. The drills are each first fitted to their stock, and then have their cutting edges formed. Any number ot drills may be fitted to and used with one drill stock. Stocks of different sizes are used according to the dimensions of the hole to be drilled. The usual sizes are

Fig 45. DRILL-STOCK.

rom two to three inches in length, having ferrules from one-quarter to three-quarters of an inch in diameter, and bored to take drills of from one-fifteenth to one-tenth ot an inch in diameter. The pointed end ot the drill-stock works in a centre punch mark on the end of the chops of the bench vice, and the tool is rotated with a drill bow. An Archimedian drill-stock sometimes takes the place of the ordinary kind.

Emery Grinders.—Shellac, melted together with emery, and fixed to a short metal rod, form a grinder used for opening the holes in enamelled dials. The grinder is generally rotated with the thumb and forefinger, and water is used to lubricate its cutting part, which soon wears away. The grinder is reshaped by heating the shellac and moulding the mass whilst it is in a plastic condition.

Endstones.—The small stone which is laid on the jewel-holes and receives the bearings of the end of the pivot ; end-stones are invariably used in the balance-axis bearings, and often throughout the escapement.

Escapements.—The escapement of a watch consists of that portion of its mechanism which regulates the speed of the train. Usually the rotary motion of the train is converted into a reciprocating motion of the balance, and it is through the escapement that this is effected. There are many varieties of escapements, but only a few are in general use. The object of the escapement is to check the rotation of the train-wheels so as to cause the force of the mainspring to remain in action for a longer period, and at the same time to regulate the rate at which the train rotates. This being the case, it is obvious that the escapement plays the most important part in regulating the going of a watch. The balance that makes its vibration perfectly isochronal will keep accurate time. Isochronism, or equal beats in equal time, is the object to be aimed at for a perfect time-keeper. Many constantly varying forces act on the mechanism of a watch and cause variation in the force carried to the escapement, and these have to be counteracted by an effective escapement with a good balance. Some escapements are particularly suitable for only special purposes, and become useless when misapplied. Obviously all escapements used for watch-work must be constructed to go equally well in the various positions in which the watch is liable to be placed. Some account should also be taken of the variation of temperature which is usually experienced by watch-work. The properties of various escapements and their imperfections and commendable features are subjects that are continually being discussed in the trade. It would be beyond our scope to treat elaborately on the intricate details of escapements generally. Neither is it proposed to examine the peculiarities of escapements that are not in general use. Upwards of a hundred different escapements could be described, but as those in general use comprise only five, these will suffice. The verge, the cylinder the duplex, the lever, and the chronometer are those which interest practical workmen. There are three classes of escapements, the above comprise specimens of each. The recoil, so named because when in action it causes the train to make a retrograde motion more or less marked. The verge belongs to this class. The dead beat escapement is one in which the escapement is perfectly at rest, a tooth of the wheel resting against the axis of the balance, except at the time the impulse is given. The cylinder and duplex escapements belong to this class. Detached escapements are dead beat also, but the balance and its axis are quite distinct from the escape-wheel, which rests against an intermediate piece except at the time the impulse is given. Lever and chronometer escapements belong to this class. The primitive verge escapement is now only a remnant of past horological art. These escapements are not now generally made, but still very many watches exist with verge escapements. It was the first employed in time-keepers, and was the only escapement known up to the middle of the seventeenth century. The verge acted without a balance-spring, and the earlier forms may be likened to the escapement now found in bottle roasting-jacks. Very good results, too, have been attained with the verge escapement ; but it has now been surpassed and modern watchmakers bestow little attention upon it.   The modern escapements are superior in their action, and the faulty theory of the verge renders it unsuitable to the perfected state of the art.   This escapement is largely affected by a small variation in the motive force, consequently the fusee is necessary, and most careful adjustment of the mainspring, so that it gives an unvarying power, is requisite to get good timekeeping qualities.   Owing to the escape-wheel being in a plane at right angles to the plates, a verge movement must necessarily be thick, and this does not accord with modern requirements. For clock-work, or in any case where the arc of vibration is small, the verge escapement is at a much better advantage. When the pivot-holes become but slightly enlarged the depthing of the escapement is altered considerably.   Also owing to the contacts of the escapement occurring when both the wheel and pallets are in motion, each travelling in opposite directions, the force of impact produces very rapid wear.   For these reasons the verge escapement is in need of constant repair.

The cylinder or horizontal escapement is the one commonly used in Geneva watches.   It is capable of considerable accuracy in time-keeping qualities, and being cheaper to produce than the lever, the cylinder escapement is extensively employed; but especially in Continental watches.   Graham invented the cylinder escapement early in the eighteenth century, but Berthold, the famous French horologist, first perfected and brought it into use.   At that time the escape-wheels were made of brass, and were very thick.   It is now adopted for the larger portion of Swiss and French watches, being cheap in construction and allowing the watch to be made very flat.   It is called a frictional-rest escapement, owing to the fact that during the whole time that the escape-wheel is at rest the point of a tooth is in contact with the cylinder. From a consideration of the action of the escapement, it will be understood that the rotation of the escape-wheel is checked by the point of the tooth resting alternately on the inner and outer surface of the cylinder. When the tooth is so resting, the balance and cylinder continue to oscillate by the force of momentum. The amount of the friction between the escape-wheel tooth and the cylinder will greatly affect the going of the watch. If the motive power of the train is increased the friction is increased, and the watch thus made to go slower. The increase of power and the increase of friction thus, to an extent, have a sort of natural compensation. In order to reduce friction, cylinders have been made of ruby; but the extra cost of labour and material is not compensated for by the questionably superior result. Though much superior to the verge, it would be wrong to suppose that the cylinder escapement is perfect; though for ordinary wear it answers. The duplex escapement is modified from the first ideas attributed to Dr. Hooke. In 1660 he made a watch for Charles II., having an escapement from which the modern duplex has been evolved. In the original there were two escape wheels, but now, the peculiar double set of teeth are cut on one wheel. The duplex-escapement is one that requires a great nicety of workmanship, and though possessed of excellent qualities, it does not approach the lever for general usefulness in every-day wear. The duplex has a frictional rest, thus resembling the cylinder. The peculiar sort of natural compensation for increased motive power exists, and, curiously, there is also a sort of natural compensation for variation of temperature. Cold weather, which, by increasing the force of the balance-spring, causes the watch to gain, also acting on the oil and increasing the adhesion of the points in

contact during frictional rest, causes a sort of natural compensation.   That these two effects absolutely neutralise each
other there is no ground for asserting, but the duplex-escapement does not require a compensation-balance in the same
degree as it is required by a lever or other detached escapement.   Owing to certain peculiarities, the duplex-escapement
is liable to set or stop when carried, and for this reason it is
not desirable in a pocket-watch.   The dead beat action of
the escapement renders it particularly suitable for dead
seconds watches, and it is for these that it is chiefly used.

The lever-escapement is now universally recognised as the
best adapted for pocket-watches where accuracy is essential.
There are many varieties of the lever-escapement, and it
would be hardly possible to enumerate all the modifications
that have been introduced.   The English lever is perhaps
the most favourably known.   This is a right-angle escapement.   The straight line lever is a variety that is used in
some high-class watches.   These terms are indicative of the
relative positions of the centres of the escape-wheel, the
pallets, and the balance.   The dead-beat escapement, invented
by Graham, and used in clocks, was the original idea of the
lever-escapement.   In order to apply it to watch-work several
important modifications were necessary.   Thomas Mudge
succeeded in producing the lever-escapement in a form that
worked satisfactorily, about the close of the eighteenth
century.   This was the detached-lever, as distinguished from
the rack-lever, which had been used by Hautefeuille.   The
escape-wheels of lever-escapements are usually made of brass,
but occasionally of steel, though this is inferior material for
the purpose.   Very hard brass is best suited for these escape-
wheels.   The form of the teeth is varied, but pointed wedge-
shaped is the form usually adopted in the English-escape-
ment.   Club teeth, as those having enlarged ends are called,

are considered advantageous, as they retain the oil on the points of action. Foreign escapements frequently have club-toothed steel wheels.

Equation Watch.—One made with two sets of hands, so that both the mean solar time and the apparent solar time may be seen.

Eye-glass.—A magnifying glass, which is greatly affected by all engaged in watch work. The lens is fitted in a cylindrical case, which is so shaped that it may be held in the eye. The edge of the eye-glass, as the entire instrument is designated, is placed beneath the eyebrow and a piece of skin lifted slightly. The opposite circumference is then allowed to lie on the upper part of the cheek— that is, just below the eye, where it will catch, and thus the eye-glass will be held securely.

Fig. 46 EYE-GLASS.

Facing-tools are used for polishing the ends or faces of pinions. These tools are usually made of soft iron ; oilstone dust and " red-stuff " being used to grind and polish with In shape a facing-tool is similar to the punches used for driving out cylinder plugs, the projecting pin being replaced by a hole in the facing-tool.

Ferrules.—Discs, with grooves in the edge, by which work may be revolved with a drill-bow. Screw ferrules are used in many cases, but plain ferrules are better in some. They are made of brass, ivory, and other material, wax serving to cement them to the object to be turned. Plain ferrules are driven on drill-spindles, arbors, &c., and form part of these tools.

Filing Block.—A block of hard wood used for filing pins on. On the edges of the block longitudinal grooves are cut, in which any wire held in the pin-vice is laid whilst being filed, the block being held in the jaws of the bench-vice. The pin-vice is twirled between the thumb and fingers of the left hand, whilst the right hand actuates the file. Filing blocks are often pieces of boxwood an inch and a half square, and half an inch thick, with grooves on each edge.

Filing or Arbor-squaring Apparatus.—This is used on the lathe to guide the file in the operations named. Three varieties of style are illustrated below.

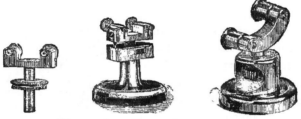

Figs. 47, 48, 49. FILING ATTACHMENTS.

Fig. 47 shows a filing attachment to be held in the hand-rest in place of the T. It is adjusted vertically, by means of a finely-threaded screw, fitted with a milled nut, as shown. The guides are hardened steel and fixed in their places: being round they may be turned over if worn by use. This attachment is useful in filing squares on arbors held between the lathe centres; the division-plate is used to divide the square correctly. Fig. 48 is a more complete apparatus, which fastens directly on the lathe-bed. The height is adjusted by means of the graduated nut. Fig. 49 is a filing fixture, made by the American Watch Tool Company. The guides for the file are hardened rollers, which may be adjusted for height by a screw and milled nut, seen in the illustration.

Fly.—An arbor carrying two wings, which, by their resistance to the atmosphere, impede the revolution of the axis and thus control the velocity of the mechanism; a fly usually regulates the striking works of repeating watches, &c.

Fly-spring.—This is the spring fitted inside the belly of the case and which causes the cover to fly up.

Fly-wheels are used, instead of bows, for driving lathes and, in some cases, for driving even drill-stocks used in the ordinary way. A continuous rotation in one direction is necessarily more economical than the alternating motion as produced by a drill bow. Fig. 50 shows a new style of foot wheel recommended for use with the lathe illustrated on page 104. It has a rocking motion to the stirrup, and its general construction may be inferred from the cut.

Fig. 50. FLY-WHEEL.

Follower.—(See " Potence.")

Fork.—The notch in the end of the lever which takes the ruby pin in the detached lever escapement.

Fourth Wheel.—That wheel of the train which drives the escape-wheel pinion, and usually carries the seconds-hand.

Frames.—The two plates, with the pillars and other parts affixed to them, are called the frames of a watch, the wheels and small work not being included by the term. Hard brass, which has been well hammered, is the material usually employed for the frames, which, after being finally finished and made smooth, are gilt for appearance sake.

Frame Saw.—A small saw, commonly known as a fret saw, fixed in a steel frame which is adjustable to the length of the saw. Clamp-screws hold the saw at its extreme ends, and one of the jaws by which the saw is held is movable and may be fixed with a clamp-screw. A bowed end affords a slight spring for the saw ; a handle at the opposite end gives the means of actuating the frame. Saws should always be fixed to cut during the pulling, not the thrust of the frame. (See " Bow-saw.")

Full-plate Watch.—Movements are so called when the top plate is a circular disc, and the balance lies above it ; when the plate is cut away to allow the balance to be sunk on to the pillar-plate, the movement becomes a three-quarter or half-plate (which see).

Fusee.—The cone-shaped cylinder, cut with a spiral groove to receive the chain ; the chain is wound off the barrel on to the fusee, and the increased tension of the spring, as it is wound further, is compensated for by acting on the smaller diameter of the cone ; thus the varying power of the spring is made to act with a uniform force on the train, and if so desired the number of turns of the mainspring may be increased through the medium of the fusee. Originally made to effect the above purpose when mainsprings were of uneven quality, the object has been latterly to an extent accomplished by the production of springs of uniform strength, so that by the judicious selection of the middle coils, the action of the two ends being prevented by stop-work, a going barrel is made to transmit a tolerably uniform force, and thus the fusee has fallen into disuse, though for a long time the characteristic of English watches.   It is still preserved in ships' chronometers, but pocket watches of even the best quality are most frequently made with a going barrel, which, when properly adjusted, is sufficiently accurate and less liable to derangement than the fusee and its appurtenances.

Fusee-turning Arbors.—These are arbors contrived for turning fusees. The arbor is made in two distinct pieces, one consists of the ferrule, having a coned point projecting. The other piece is a steel rod, about an inch and a half long, split down the centre, nearly its entire length. The divided part is fitted with screws to form jaws to hold on to the fusee square. The other end is fitted with a disc, which is attached to the ferrule in such a way that the two pieces may be moved at right angles to the axis of rotation. By this arrangement, when a fusee is gripped by the square in the jaws, the arbor can be shifted so as to make the fusee run true.

Geneva Stop.—The Maltese cross form of stopwork applied to all going barrel watches. (See "Stopwork.")

Glossing.—A process of finishing brass effected with red-stuff. Scrupulous cleanliness is essential to success in all polishing operations, but more especially in glossing. The red-stuff used is a fine, soft quality, and is applied, mixed with oil, with elder pith. A good black gloss should be attained by these means. A little rouge mixed with the red-stuff will assist in attaining the result; but the polish will not be so durable.

Going Barrel.—A mainspring barrel having teeth cut on its periphery which gear direct into the centre pinion, thus doing away with the chain and fusee; it is used chiefly in foreign watches, though recently the going barrel is employed more generally and in the finest class of work. (See "Fusee.")

Gravers.—These are used for turning, and resemble the same tools used in other trades for the same purpose. They are of square and lozenge section, and are named after their form. The largest used in watch-work seldom exceed one-tenth of an inch across the flat.

Great Wheel.—The wheel on the base of the fusee which drives the centre pinion.

Greying.—A process of finishing brass effected by water-of-Ayr stone. The stone is filed flat and charged with clean oil; an even grey surface is attained by a polishing process. Bright grey finish is a continuation of the process, using rottenstone on a wood slip.

Hairspring.—(See "Balance Spring.")

Half-plate Watches.—Those in which the upper plate approximately resembles a half circle; in them the fourth wheel is generally planted in a cock. The term is used analogously with three-quarter-plate watch (which see.)

Hammers.—Those used in watch-work differ but little,

Fig. 51. HAMMER.

except in size, from many that are employed by other handicraftsmen. The largest commonly used weighs but an ounce and a half, and frequently hammer heads that weigh only a quarter of an ounce are to be found on the watchmaker's bench. Steel heads are the most common; those having round faces are for riveting. Brass and other soft metals are used for making hammer heads that are to be used on finished work. The handle is generally about ten inches long, and very small near the end where the head is fixed, so as to make it springy.

Hand Tongs.—Tools similar to sliding tongs but having jaws specially constructed to hold watch hands, so that

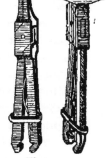

Figs. 52, 53
HAND-TONGS.

they may be conveniently shaped to fit on the motion work. There are two forms of hand-tongs in general use. One has narrow jaws, with slits to hold the hands, shaped to give the choice of two sizes. The other form has jaws over an inch wide, pierced with holes to hold the hour-hands, and having slots for the minute-hands.

Hand-vice.—This tool is but a diminutive form of the ordinary hand-vice used by many workers in metal. It is seldom

54. HAND-VICE.

that a watch repairer requires this tool, the pin-vice or sliding tongs answering most purposes, except for particularly large work, for which the bench-vice is generally available.

Hardening.—A process by which metals are made harder. Steel has the peculiar property of becoming exceedingly hard if cooled suddenly when at a red heat. It is this property that renders steel so valuable for making cutting tools, &c. Care must be exercised to guard against overheating the steel which will injure it. Oil or water are most commonly used for cooling, but any method of suddenly extracting the heat will be effective After hardening, the steel will require to be tempered, which process is described under its heading. Brass can be hardened by hammering or rolling; heat causes it to become soft.

Hour Wheel.—One of the motion wheels, which fits on the cannon-pinion and carries the hour-hand.

Hunting Cases.—Those which have a metal cover to protect the glass over the dial.

Independent Seconds Watch.—This has two independent trains of wheels driven by separate mainsprings. One train drives a seconds-hand, which may be stopped at any time without interfering with the other train which drives the ordinary set of hands. For greater exactness in timing, watches are made to indicate fractions of seconds, most frequently fourths or fifths, and the seconds-hand may be stopped at these fractional parts of a second. (See also "Centre Seconds.")

Index.—The point of the regulator which is moved to cause the watch to go faster or slower—fast and slow, or advance and retard, usually abbreviated to the initial letters of these words, being engraved on the surface near the index to indicate the direction in which this should be moved. Any pointer used to indicate is termed an index when not one of the hands.

H

Jacot Tool.—The Jacot tool is used for finishing the pivots after they have been turned nearly to size and shape in the turns. Some watchmakers use the turns only, and finish the pivots with a graver, only using red stuff to polish them with finally; but in the Jacot tool it is usual to use a pivoting file.

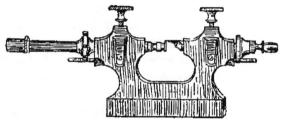

Fig. 55 JACOT-TOOL

With this the pivot is reduced in size, and at the same time made quite parallel. A similarly shaped file, without any teeth, called a pivot burnisher, is next applied, and with this the final burnish or polish is put on the pivots. The Jacot tool has one centre, of which both ends may be used, one being for treating the diameter of the pivots only, the other for reducing their length and rounding up the ends. The end used for the first operation has about a dozen facets on it, each having a semi-circular groove in the centre, and these grooves are graduated

Figs 56, 57. JACOT-TOOL CENTRES.

in size to suit all the usual run of watch pivots. In use, first select one of the large grooves and place it uppermost; then put the pinion to be operated on against the left female centre, with the pivot to be finished lying n the groove of the opposite centre, this being adjusted to very nearly touch the shoulder; then lay the pivoting file on the pivot to keep it in the groove, and with the drill-bow revolve the pinion, at the same time moving the file backwards and forwards. This is continued till the diameter of the pivot is reduced to a level with the face of the groove on which the file rests; and if it is desired to still further reduce the size of the pivot, the Jacot centre must be moved on one division to the next size smaller, and so on till the pivot is of the size required. In every case great care must be taken to keep the edge of the file into the corner of the pivot, so that the shoulder will be left square; and after the file is discarded the burnisher must be used to finish the pivot with. When the shoulder of the pivot is small, and the file apt to slip along the axis, as for instance with a verge, which would be broken through the pallet catching against the file, it is customary to use a guard-piece, which is sold with the Jacot tool. This is fixed on to the centre, and has a small finger projecting just above the diameter of the centre, and close against its end, forming a rest for the edge of the file. In the hands of an inexperienced pivoter this guard-piece will be found to prevent many slips and consequent breakages, but with practice its use may be dispensed with except in special cases. The reverse end of the principal centre of the Jacot tool is generally protected with a brass cap, as it has a very thin edge, pierced with holes of graduating size, corresponding with the sizes of pivots. In use, the pivot to be operated on is put to work in a hole which nearly fits it, so that the end of the centre bears against the shoulder, and the point of the pivot thus left projecting is shaped and burnished by means of very small half-round files, about an inch long, and correspondingly small. Another centre sometimes forms part of a Jacot tool. This is only single ended, and has three or four grooves in it, specially made for treating long-seconds pivots, the grooves being longer, and the faces cuts lightly tapering to make the pivot a trifle conical. For turning the work in a Jacot tool, use a weak bow with a horse-hair, and for pinions which have the wheels fixed on them, instead of using an ordinary screw ferrule, a plain brass ferrule, having a large hole in the centre, or even better still, one of ivory, with a little beeswax melted on one side, will be found much more convenient. Such a furrule is fixed quite firmly enough for all ordinary purposes by simply pressing it on to the side of the wheel, the arms of which embed themselves in the wax.

Jewel Holes.—Used instead of bushes in the more delicate bearings of watches; all the bearings of the escapement are usually jewelled, and sometimes the train as far as the centre wheel. Ruby jewel holes are the best, being hardest, but inferior stones are more frequently employed. Jewelled bearings are more durable than metal even though this be of the hardest, and the friction in them is less; hence their invariable use in all high-class work.

Jewel Screwdrivers.—Very diminutive screwdrivers, made of small steel wire and fitted into a wire handle, used for turning jewel screws.

Jewelling Cutter.—This tool, shown at Figs. 58 to 63, is

Fig. 59. CENTRE.

Fig 60. CUTTER STOCK.

a time-saving device, cutting jewel settings in a few seconds. Sets of twelve, with gauge, are packed in a box and sold complete; they are specially adapted for use in the American lathes, and the usual size fits No. 38 chuck. The faces numbered 10 and 12 form the bezel, which can be made heavier if desired by grinding from face 10. These cutting faces may be

Fig. 58. JEWEL SETTER.

sharpened when dull. The tool is used like an ordinary drill, feeding the work with the back centre. A small hole first made, large enough to admit the point of the cutter, which gradually reams the hole and so gives steadiness and prevents a too rapid feed, which would injure the cutter and work.

Fig 61 Stop Colllar.

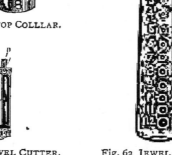

Fig 62. Jewel Cutter,   Fig. 63 Jewel Gauge

Joint Pusher.—A round steel pin fitted into a handle and used to push the joint pins out of watch cases. It is a very simple tool, the pin being of a size convenient for the hole through the joint, and having its end filed flat.

Key Gauge.—This is a disc of brass with several steel squares projecting from it radially. These squares being graduated in size, form gauges on which to try the sizes of key pipes. Twelve sizes are now generally recognised, but as the largest and smallest are variously taken as the commencing size, which may be 1 or oo, and as this size is purely arbitrary, it is impossible to give any tangible equivalent for the value of key sizes.

Keyless Mechanism.—This is an arrangement for winding the watch without the aid of an independent key. The most usual is that of a steel shaft passing through the centre of the pendant and having a serrated knob fitted to its top, by which it may be turned by means of the finger and thumb. The end, which is in the interior of the case, is fitted with gearing to connect it with the winding square, the particular method being determined by many reasons. Invariably the same gearing is used for setting the hands, it being thrown in gear by applying pressure to a small projection provided for the purpose on the circumference of the case. When used in fusee watches, the mechanism must spring out of gear automatically as the winding square revolves during the going of the watch. The advantages of keyless mechanism are obviously the convenience of always having the key with the watch, and with it the cases do not require to be opened, and hence may fit tighter, making them the less pervious to dust and moisture.

Lathes.—The application of the lathe to watch work is of comparatively recent date. The last ten years has seen the development of the application, but, previously, the lathe, as the term is now understood, was but little used in general watch work, though, for special purposes, the tool has been employed since the early days of horology. The accompanying illustrations show lathes with various attachments, from which much useful information may be inferred. For many purposes, and especially for light work, watchmaker's lathes will be found particularly useful. The machines are somewhat costly, being made with great accuracy and of first-rate material, though small in comparison with mechanics' lathes generally.

The Moseley lathe is shown as a specimen of the modern American lathe used in watch work. Mr. C. S Moseley has been connected with the manufacture of watches by machinery from its infancy in America, and was the first to bring into use the split or spring chuck, in its present form; was also the original superintendent, and for five years designing and consulting engineer of the Elgin National Watch Company, of Elgin, Ill., U.S.A. He originated and perfected many appliances for producing these tools. The Moseley lathe is made in three sizes and two qualities. The sizes are: No. 1, length of bed nine-and-a-half inches, height of centre one-and-three-

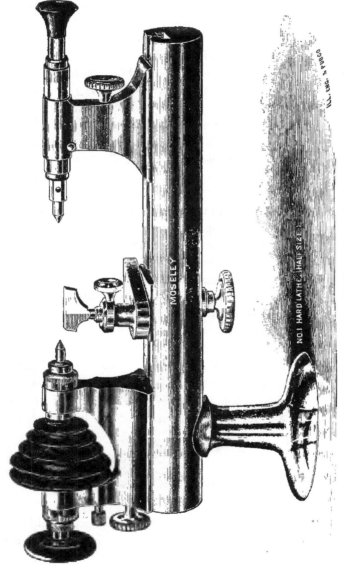

Fig. 64. Moseley's No. 1 Hard Lathe.

quarter inches; No. 2, length of bed eleven inches, height of centre two inches; No. 3, length of bed fifteen inches, height of centre three-and-three-eighths inches. The No. 1 lathe illustrated is half size (Fig. 64), has a bed nine-and-a-half inches long, height of centre one-and-three-quarter inches, so that it swings three-and-a-half inches, and costs £10. In the hard lathes the head and tailstock, spindles and their bushings, are of the finest-tempered *steel*, ground to size and shape by special machinery. The outside surface of entire lathe is highly polished and nickel-plated, cone pulleys of hard rubber with four speed changes, and indexed with sixty holes, that a circle may be divided in 60, 30, 20, 15, 12, 10, 6, 5, 4, 3, or 2 equal divisions. The bearings on all lathes have *oil holes* and *oil chambers* in the bushings, covered by shields which exclude chips and dust and protect the operator from flying oil. An opening in the shield allows the bearing to be lubricated, and by a partial revolution closes the opening, confining the oil where it is needed, without the usual cup and its cover, which is continually being misplaced.

The headstock is fastened to the bed by a bolt at each end in combination with wedges and screws, which makes it very secure and easily attached or detached. The tailstock is fitted with hardened sliding spindle and bushings; rear end mounted with hard rubber knob, and taper hole in front for centres, drill chucks, &c. Fig. 65 shows a section of the bed adopted in

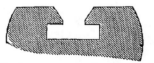

Fig 65 SECTION OF LATHE-BED.

the Moseley lathe. It has central guiding surfaces, which are more correct in principle than to spread the guides to the outside. The screw for binding T in rest is tapped in a steel

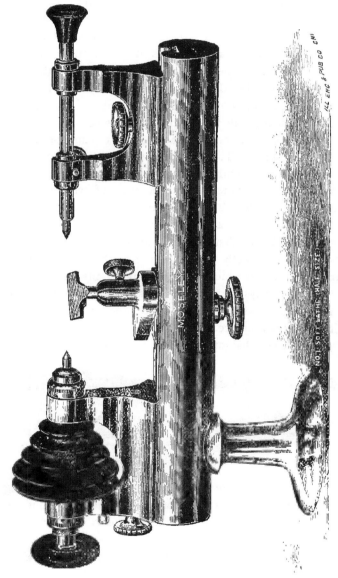

Fig. 66. MOSELEY'S NO. 1 SOFT LATHE.

ring, which can be set in any position, thus accommodating all workmen and all work.

The sliding shoe has an arrangement by which it is held down on the bed to prevent chips and dust from collecting under, at the same time allowing it to move perfectly free. The lathes are fastened to bench by a heavy wood screw, leaving all clear below, or by bolt and thumb nut beneath the bench. The many calls for something at less cost has induced the make of a lathe without hardened bearings—same perfection in all working parts. They are in style nearly the same as just described, the live mandrel or spindle running in anti-friction metal bearings, steel work soft, except mouth of live spindle and the tail-stock spindle. The pulley indexed; twenty-four holes. By the use of a new and expensive machine all head and tail-stocks and all other fixtures are made interchangeable, every centre of exactly same height from bed, and perfectly central. No matter which way they may be placed upon the bed they will always line correctly, thus obviating the necessity of purchasing a complete outfit at once, and permit of making additions at convenience.

Fig. 67 shows a half-open tail-stock. The upper half is cut

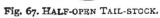

Fig. 67. HALF-OPEN TAIL-STOCK.   Fig. 68. TRAVERSE SPINDLE.

away so that spindles may be laid in place, instead of being passed through. This is very convenient when a number of spindles are to be used for drilling, tapping, counterboring, chamfering, &c.

Fig. 68 is a traverse spindle tail-stock useful for straight drilling.   Fig. 69 shows a very light-running spindle used for

lapping, pivoting, jewel polishing, and any other kind of light, work requiring high speed.   Fig. 74 shows a screw tail-stock useful for heavy wor

The Universal Head, shown half-size at Fig. 71, has the face-plate only three-and-a-half inches diameter, but by the use of two crescent-shaped slots will hold anything in size and

Fig. 69
LIGHT-RUNNING SPINDLE.

shape of watch-work, putting to shame heavy and clumsy tools, which can do no more.   The pump centre is operated from back end by rubber knob ; and is used either with or without a spring.   Jaws are held in position on face-plate by springs and fastened from the back, which is considered most desirable ; the jaws will pass the centre.   They are compact in form and

Fig. 70. SCREW TAIL-STOCK.

pleasant to handle, while the clamps project the least possible distance above the work.

The Whitcomb lathe, manufactured by the American Watch Tool Company, is shown at Fig. 72.   It is claimed for this lathe that it embraces all the improvements suggested by the experience of the best watch repairers in America. All its lines have been studied to combine beauty with strength and convenience. Its size and proportions secure solidity which prevents vibration. The production of the Whitcombe lathe has increased from twenty-five lathes in 1874 to two hundred and eighty-five in 1881. The lathe is made

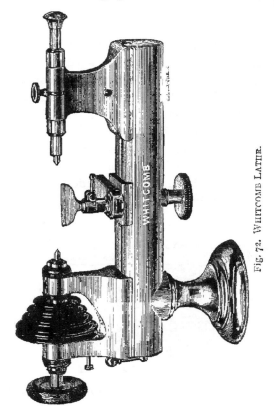

Fig. 72. WHITCOMB LATHE.

in three sizes. No. 1 has the bed seven seven-eights of an inch long, and swings three one-eighths of an inch. No. 1½ has the bed nine and three-quarters of an inch, and swings nearly four inches. No. 2 has the bed eleven and seven-eighths of an inch, and swings four and three-quarters of an inch. These dimensions are only approximate, as the lathes are made to metric measurements.

Fig. 71. UNIVERSAL HEAD.

Each lathe has a plain tail-stock and hand-rest, as shown in Fig. 72; the cost varies with the size. Also, two distinct

Fig. 73. UNIVERSAL HEAD,

qualities are made, a *soft* and a *hard* lathe. The price of the one and a half lathe is, for the former, about £8, and for the latter about £12.

Fig. 73 shows the Universal Head, which every watchmaker will easily identify. Near the centre are shown three taper peep-holes, through which the action of the pumping centre may be observed. This is a decided advantage. The method of operating the clamps is similar to that adopted in Swiss mandrels, though some improvements are claimed for it.

Fig 74. Screw Tail-stock.

Fig. 74 is a screw tail-stock, made much heavier than the one shown in Fig. 72, and useful for heavy drilling.

Lepine Movements.—So called from their originator and principal manufacturer. Their chief characteristics are extreme flatness, and the wheels are invariably pivoted in bars and cocks. These improvements (?) were introduced in 1776, before which time fusees were in vogue. Lepine dispensed with the fusee, the chain, and one plate.

Lever.—The piece by which the balance of a lever watch receives its motion from the escapement. It is fixed to the pallets, and the pallet staff is its centre of motion. The end next the balance-staff is forked to receive the ruby pin, to which it gives the impulse derived from the action of the escape-wheel teeth on the pallets.

Lid Winding Watch.—One of the forms of case winding contrivances, in which the opening of the cover causes the spring to be partially wound up. Hunting cases are most frequently adapted to this form of winding, but it has no practical value, and is but very seldom found.

Locking Faces.—These are the faces of the pallets in all kinds of escapements which lock the escape-wheel during the supplementary arc of the balance.

Mainspring.—A long ribbon of steel, which, coiled in the barrel, forms the motive power of watchwork. The introduction of the mainspring in place of the weight formerly used may be considered to mark the birth of watches or portable clocks. It would appear that this occurred about the middle of the sixteenth century. The fusee was introduced almost simultaneously, as the inequalities of the mainsprings first produced were such as to render a fusee necessary. Gut lines were originally employed to transmit the power.

Mainspring Punch.—A tool for punching holes through mainsprings for the purpose of making the eye, or for making a hole to affix a hook. The tool is usually made somewhat

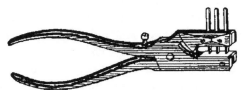

Fig. 75. Mainspring Punch.

like a pair of pliers, with the jaws about half an inch apart. One jaw is fitted with punches, often three or four of different sizes, and the other jaw has a steel plate with holes forming dies.

Mainspring Winder.—This instrument is used to coil up a mainspring before putting it in the barrel. It consists of a brass frame carrying a shaft, which may be turned with a winch handle, fitted with a ratchet and click. One end of the shaft has a nose fitted with a hook similar to a barrel arbor

The inner end of the mainspring is hooked on to the nose,
and the shaft is turned by the winch till the spring is entirely
coiled, then the barrel is put over it. The ratchet wheel has

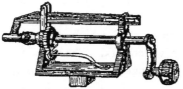

Fig 76. Mainspring Winder

Fig. 77. Chucks for Main-
spring Winder

angular teeth, and the click is reversible, so that the spring
may be wound either way.

Maintaining Power.—In fusee watches, when the arbor
of the fusee is turned by the key in winding in the direction
opposite to the force of the spring, the whole of this force is
absorbed in the power expended in winding, and the fusee is
turned in the backward direction, and the train would go
backwards but for the intervention of a contrivance called the
maintaining power. Some old verge watches are still met with
having no maintaining power, and which consequently run
backwards whilst being wound. The maintaining power consists of a steel wheel, with ratchet-shaped teeth, on the arbor,
between the body and the fusee and the great wheel. This
steel wheel carries the clicks which engage in the teeth of the
fusee-ratchet wheel, by which the winding is effected. The
great wheel has a hollow turned in its thickness for the recep-
tion of a flat steel spring, called the maintaining power spring,
which is circular in form, one end being secured to the great
wheel, the other free end engaging with the steel ratchet wheel ;
the action of this spring being restrained by a slot cut in the
great wheel. The power of the mainspring first overcomes the
resistance of the maintaining power spring, and, having drawn
this as far as the slot will allow, then causes the fusee to rotate.

The steel wheel is prevented from turning in the direction contrary to the one by which the great wheel communicates motion to the centre pinion by means of the detent (which see), so that when the fusee arbor is turned by the key the steel wheel is stopped by the detent, and the maintaining power spring exerts its force in turning the great wheel, and keeping the watch going. The action of this spring is of sufficient duration to keep the train going for several minutes, and each time that the power turning the fusee arbor is relaxed, and the mainspring allowed to exert its force, the maintaining power spring is again wound up fully. The going fusee, or maintaining power, was invented by Harrison, the maker of the chronometer which gained the Government award of £20,000. Going barrels require no such contrivance, as in winding the power of the mainspring is in no way taken from the periphery of the barrel.

Mandrel.—This is a peculiar kind of lathe which is confined to the watchmaking trade. The head-stock is arranged for holding a watch movement by the plate, which is gripped in jaws which always hold it quite in flat. The centre of the mandrel is furnished with a sliding cylindrical steel rod having a pointed end. This point is placed in the hole around which it is desired to turn, and the plate is clamped in that position. Thus any hole may be made to form the centre of the work. Figs. 37, 71 and 73 illustrate the chief feature of a mandrel.

Minute Wheel.—One of the motion wheels which transmits the motion of the cannon-pinion to the hour-wheel.

Motion Wheels.—The set of wheels which drive the hands, comprising the cannon-pinion, the minute-wheel, and the hour wheel. The cannon-pinion drives the minute-wheel, and carries on it the hour-wheel, which is driven by the pinion of the minute-wheel, so that both hour and minute hands revolve from the same centre and in the same direction, the relative velocity being always arranged in the gearing to produce twelve turns of the cannon-pinion to one of the hour-wheel. The whole are also called the motion work.

Movement Holder.—A contrivance for holding watch movements whilst they are being put together. Three jaws close on the pillar-plate and grip it tightly, the frame of which they form part, forming a stand which is convenient for handling by.

Nippers.—Cutting pliers used for cutting wire and many other purposes, as nipping off the points of hands which are

Figs. 78, 79 NIPPERS.

too long. Nippers generally have the jaws parallel to the joint, but sometimes they are made at an angle with it.

Oil Cups.—Receptacles for oil used on the bench Only very small quantities of oil, merely a few drops, are required for the general purposes of oiling watch-work, and oil-cups are used to contain it.

Oiler.—A small piece of fine brass, usually fitted into a wire a handle. It should be filed down, very fine and then slightly flattened at the point, so as to take up a very minute quantity of oil, used for oiling the watch.

Open Face Case.—Those which have a glass only over the dial, so that the time is seen without opening the case in any way.

Pallets.—The parts on which the escape-wheel teeth fall. That piece in a lever watch which embraces some of the escape-wheel teeth, and translates the circular motion of the escape-wheel, through the lever, into the vibratory motion of the balance. The faces of the pallets are jewelled when the escape-wheel teeth come in contact. Those portions of a verge which receive the impulse from the escape-wheel are also called pallets, and generally those parts which perform analogous functions in different escapements.

Pegwood.—A small underwood known as wild cornal or dogwood, and used for cleaning the pivot and other holes in watch-work in preference to other woods, owing to its being remarkably free from silex and pith. For cleaning pivot holes a stick is pointed at one end like a pencil, except that less pains are taken to make the cone smooth and regular. Three cuts are made, commencing at about half an inch from the end, so as to form a triangular pyramid. The apex is inserted in the hole to be cleaned, and the peg of wood twirled in alternate directions by the fingers and thumb, used precisely as in actuating the screwdriver, except that the index finger assists the middle and third fingers instead of resting on the top of the stick. The other end is cut off in three facets, and the obtuse pyramid thus formed is used to clean out the counter-sunk oil-holes. The wood is continually cut at both ends, and thus new and clean points are made till only an inch or so of the stick is left, and it becomes too short for further use. The simple process of cutting the wood to a sharp point is not to be done without practice, as the extreme point of the pyramid must be very fine, and still perfectly firm, so that it can be got in the fine pivot holes. A freshly-sharpened peg is generally used first in the smallest hole and then through the larger, till finally the largest hole is cleaned, before the peg is resharpened ; and the process is repeated till the clean peg fails to show discoloration when twirled in the holes.

Pendant.—That part which is soldered into the rim of the case, and to which the bow is attached. The pendant usually contains the push piece, by which pressure from the thumb is communicated to the lock spring, which releases the case and allows it to fly open.

Pendant Winder.—The mechanism which enables a watch to be wound from the pendant. It usually consists of an arbor through the centre of the pendant, and having a fluted button on the outer end. The inner end is connected with wheels, to wind up the mainspring, and by pressing a push piece, or in some cases the button itself, the hands may be actuated instead. By adopting this mechanism, all the trouble of providing a watch-key is avoided. The case need not be opened for winding, and hence there is less chance of dust getting to the movement. Most of the better class watches are now provided with keyless mechanism (which see).

Pendulum Spring.—See "Balance Spring."

Pillar Plate.—The plate in which the pillars are riveted, invariably the one next the dial, and on which the entire movement of a watch is based.

Pillars.—The columns, usually three or four, which have one end riveted into one of the plates, called the pillar-plate, and at the other end a shoulder, against which the other or top-plate rests, this latter plate being secured by screws put in longitudinally or pins put transversely. The pillars serve to keep the two plates at a uniform distance apart, and should be of precisely equal length.

Pin Slide—A tool which answers the ordinary purpose of

Fig. 80. PIN SLIDE.

a pin-vice, but has not such a tight grip. The jaws are held together by a sliding ring.

Pin Vice.—This tool may be considered as a very diminutive form of the ordinary leg-bench vice, commonly used by engineers and various other workers in metal   The pin vice is usually about five inches in length, with jaws that are generally closed with a winged nut.   The tailed part forms a handle by which the vice is held.   The name is probably derived from the fact that the vice is used chiefly for holding wire when making pins for various purposes, as pinning the plates of a watch together.   The tail or handle is generally bored through

Fig. 81. PIN VICE.

to receive a supply of wire, and the pins are made on a filing block.   Pin vices are usualyl made of steel, and some have jaws, of the shape common to most vices, about three-quarters of an inch wide, but more often they are " dog-nosed," only about a quarter of an inch wide, the outer part being all that is wanted for holding pin wire.   There is generally a small groove in the middle of each jaw in which the wire is held central.   An expert workman can file, on the filing block, by means of a pin vice very truly.   The tool is rotated by means of the left hand whilst the file is held in the right.

Pinion Gauge.—A diminutive form of spring calliper

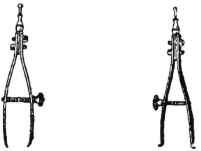

Fig. 82. PINION GAUGE.   Fig 83 HEIGHT GAUGE.

adjustable by means of a screw and milled nut.   The too

resembles a draughtsman's spring bow compass, with the leg shaped to suit gauging purposes. It is used for measuring every description of work ; but especially for gauging the length and diameter of pinions and other axes during the process of turning.

Pinion Stake.—A strip of steel or brass having a series of holes through it graduating in size. The stake is generally formed so that it may be held conveni-ently in the jaws of the bench vice, though it is commonly used lying on the bench. In use, the pinion stake supports

Fig. 84. PINION STAKE

a pinion, its arbor passing through a hole of convenient size, while the wheel is being riveted on, or a similar operation performed.

Pivot Broaches.—Very small broaches shaped like the ordinary kind, but often finer than human hair.

Pivot Drills.—Very small drills consisting of a steel shaft about an inch-and-a-half long, provided with a brass

Fig. 85. PIVOT DRILL.

ferrule about a quarter of an inch in diameter. The end is shaped like a drill, and is used to drill very small holes, as those for the pivots of the smaller axes in watch work.

Pivot Gauge.—For gauging the diameters of pivots. The tool consists of two strips of steel riveted together at both ends with a tapering slit between them.

Pivot Polishing.—Some apparatus for this purpose are fitted to lathes.

Fig. 86 is a pivot polishing fixture to fit on the slide-rest, used for grinding or polishing conical or straight pivots. It is also useful for snailing and drilling. The base is graduated so that the spindle may be set at any required angle.

Fig. 86. PIVOT POLISHER.

Fig. 87 shows another style of pivot polisher. It will do all kinds of pivots, besides spotting, snailing and drilling. It is fastened to the bed as a slide-rest, and has graduated angular and vertical adjustments. The illustration shows the attachment half-size, and the following are directions for its use. After the pivot is turned to a proper shape, put on the polisher; the spindle being parallel with the lathe-bed, and the lap to

Fig. 87. PIVOT POLISHER.

the rear. Use a cast-iron lap first, one having square corners for square shoulders, or one with round corners for conical shoulders. The lap itself must be perfectly true and uniformly smooth. Fine oilstone powder and oil, or No. 1 crocus, should be used with the iron laps. When the pivot is ground to shape, carefully clean it and remove the iron lap. Polish with a boxwood lap and No. 4 crocus.

Pliers.—These are well-known tools used in many trades. Those used for watchwork have some special features to adapt them to their special purposes. Long-nosed and short-nosed are varieties of the ordinary shape. Very long-nosed pliers having slender jaws, an inch-and-a-half long, are called follower pliers, their purpose being to mani-pulate the follower of verge watches. Snipe-nosed pliers have the outsides of the jaws rounded, and half round inside pliers have the insides of the jaws rounded, each serving the purpose of ordinary round-nosed pliers for outside and inside work respectively. Round-nosed pliers have their jaws round in section and usually tapering.

Fig 88 PLIERS.

Polishing Block.—A box fitted with an arrangement for holding polishing materials. Usually it consists of a series of about four or six turned boxwood boxes, the upper ones forming a lid for the one next beneath it, and having a bright iron surface on which the polishing material, made glutinous with oil, is kept. A tier of such boxes should be furnished with the various abrasive materials used in watch work.

Potence.—The cock which forms the lower bearing of the balance staff or verge. It is screwed to the upper plate, and in the verge watch also forms the bearing for the front pivot of the escape-pinion or swing wheel axis. The pivot holes of the balance axis are invariably jewelled, and the endstone in the potence is sometimes set in a slip of brass, and fits a dove-tailed slide in the potence. This is called the potence slip. The potence follower, used in verge watches only, is the bear-ing of the back end of the escape-pinion. It passes through a brass stud riveted in the top plate, the hole for the potence follower being drilled parallel to the surface of the plate and in a line with the swing-wheel pivot hole in the potence. By the adjustment of this follower, the depthing of the escape-wheel with the verge is regulated. For this purpose specially made pliers, with long slender jaws, are used; these are called follower pliers.

Pump Dividers.—A somewhat elaborate kind of dividers or compasses. The centre in the handle may be adjusted to protrude any required amount; that is, it pumps. The other centre, or rather cutting point, is adjustable by means of a screw, so that the distance apart may be regulated to great exactness.

Punches.—Innumerable punches are used for various purposes incidental to repairing watch work. Some have round faces for closing holes, some are bored up for riveting, and others are variously shaped to suit particular purposes. It is scarcely feasible to attempt an enumeration of all the punches even commonly used. Sets are sold in boxes containing one, two, or three dozen.

Rack Lever.—A peculiar old-fashioned lever escapement, having the end of the lever cut with teeth, the balance axis being a pinion gearing into the segment. It is said to be the invention of the Abbé Hautefeuille, in 1722, and that F. Berthoud used this escapement in some of his marine time-keepers. This form is now obsolete, being superseded by the detached lever, but prior to the introduction of this rack levers were made. Two kinds were used, one having an ordinary train and another without a fourth wheel.

Ratchet.—The wheel in which the click acts. It is generally made of steel, having a square hole in the centre, the teeth being cut angularly to receive the click, by which motion is permitted only in one direction. In some foreign watches the ratchet wheel is solid with the barrel arbor, and in the English fusee it is made of brass, and secured to the base of the fusee cone by two brass pins put in vertically.

Recoil Escapements.—This class of escapement differs from the dead beat, inasmuch as the escape wheel is driven backwards by the pallet face during the time that the balance is describing its supplementary arc ; when the face of the pallet cannot be made concentric with its axis the result is a recoil escapement, of which the verge is the only type usually met with.

Repeating Watches.—These are made to strike on a bell or wire gong the time as shown by the hands ; to effect this the repeating movement is wound up by pressing a push piece or moving a slide on the circumference of the case, and, on running down, the time is indicated by blows as above mentioned. Some strike the hours and quarters only, others the half quarters in addition, and others strike the minutes after the hours and quarters. The object of a repeating watch is to indicate the time in the dark, or to one who is blind ; but the complicated nature of the mechanism necessary to produce a result which is of comparatively little general value, renders the cost too high to make the use of repeaters extensive.

Riveting Tool.—This is a tool made to hold the punches ordinarily used for riveting, in such a manner that they may be applied to the work quite vertically.

Roller.—The circular steel collet which is fitted to a level staff, duplex staff, &c., and carries the ruby pin.

Rounding-up Tool.—Used for rounding up—that is, equalising and shaping the teeth of wheels. The tool, or rather machine, is a kind of miniature wheel-cutting engine, and is seldom found amongst the appliances of an ordinary watch-jobber.

Ruby Pin.—The pin in the roller of a lever staff which acts in the fork of the lever and receives the impulse from the escapement. Ruby pins are commonly made of a species of glass. To tighten a ruby pin, set the ruby pin in asphaltum varnish. It will become hard in a few minutes, and be much firmer and better than gum shellac, as generally used.

Screwdrivers.—These implements used for watchwork are generally cylindrical rods of from three inches to four inches in length. The shaft is frequently made of pinion wire, though a lighter material, such as some hard wood, is more desirable A collet is put to the top end, to form a rest for the index finger, by which the screwdriver is kept up to its work. The shaft is turned round by means of the thumb and middle finger, between which it is rolled. In order to afford a good grip for the finger and thumb, pinion wire or some such corrugated material is used to make the shaft. The blades of these screwdrivers are very like the ordinary carpenter's bradawl. Sometimes they are solid with the shaft, and sometimes the shaft is arranged for interchangeable blades. For very small screws, such as jewel screws, the width of the blade is about one-fiftieth of an inch. The largest blades are rarely wider than one-tenth of an inch. Between these limits there are all sizes. Three or four screwdrivers, of different sizes, are usually found on a well-ordered bench.

Screw-end Finisher.—For the purpose of holding screws so that their ends or points may be finished or polished.

Fig. 90 SCREW-END FINISHER   Fig. 91 CHUCKS FOR SCREW-END FINISHER

The same tool is used for holding seconds-hands so that their cannons may be shortened.

Screw Extractor.—A tool for removing the threaded part of screws, which are often broken off in holes. The tool consists of a U-shaped arm having through its arms near to the ends, two screws with their ends precisely opposite each other. The ends of these screws are pointed somewhat, but they are flat on the extreme end. The two ends are screwed tightly against the broken screw, and thus a grip is obtained which often enables the piece to be extracted easily when other methods fail.

Screw Ferrules.—A particular kind of ferrule adapted for screwing on to work to be mounted on the turns. The ferrule has a groove in which the cord of the bow works. Ordinary screw ferrules are made of steel, and are cut in two diametrically; the two halves are then held together by means of screws. In the centre there is a hole which must be smaller in diameter than the work to be gripped. By slacking the screws the two halves come apart, and the work is placed in the hole above mentioned. On tightening the screws the ferrule nips with a vice-like grip, and runs sufficiently true if there is not much difference between the diameter of the

Fig 92. Screw Ferrule.

central hole and that of the work. The two halves are, however, always more or less separated, and the edges cut and fray the cord. Some screw ferrules—especially those for large work—have a large hole in the centre, and three or four screws put in radially, the points of which pinch the work. Screw ferrules are made all sizes from about one-fifth of an inch in diameter —used for turning verges and such light work—to about three-quarters of an inch diameter, which is large enough for the heaviest work that is usually mounted on watchmakers' turns.

Screw Head Tool.—Used for finishing the heads of screws used in watch work. The tool consists of a frame, which is clamped in the bench-vice, and several appliances for holding the screws. These appliances are differently shaped to suit various purposes. Some are very like pin vices actuated by a sliding ring; their purpose is to clip screws by the thread whilst the heads are being operated upon. Others are arranged to hold the screws so that their points may be shaped and polished. The frame of the tool is clamped in the bench-vice in a slanting or nearly upright position, and the appliance holding a screw is placed in the frame. By rubbing the palm and fingers of the left hand on the handle part of the appliance it is turned to and fro. The right hand holds a file or other tool, which is rested against a steel pin projecting from the top of the frame. By this means the file may be steadied and brought to bear squarely on the screw head. For polishing the heads of screws especially, flat pieces called lapidaries are fitted on the steel pin. These lapidaries have surfaces of metal specially prepared for polishing, and they are kept square with the work by being fitted on the projecting steel pin.

Screw Plates.—Used for cutting the threads on screws. The screw-plates used in watchwork are the same in principle and construction to those commonly used in many other trades. For watchwork, however, only very small screws and correspondingly small screw-plates are used. Screws are made by machinery, and sold so cheaply that making them by hand is now an obsolete custom, and only when some screw of unusual form is required does the use of a screw-plate become essential. The taps necessary for screwing the holes are usually sold with machine-made screws. Most of the screw-plates used in watchwork come from the Continent.

Self-Winding Watches.—In these watches, a weighted lever, held up by a spring, is attached to a winding square in such a manner that on oscillating the lever the watch is wound, the requisite motion being imparted during the time the wearer is walking. Such a contrivance finds no favour in practice, as the watch would fail to go through not being wound should it remain still for a day, a circumstance of frequent occurrence from various causes. Occasionally such a watch is found, but generally in the cabinet of a collector of curios. The term is sometimes applied, though quite erroneously, to keyless watches.

Sizes of Watches.—It is very doubtful how small or how large watches have been made, but in general use the small size lady's watch is about a ten size, and the large size gent's watch a twenty-two size. These represent the limits of size in common use, but watches both smaller or larger are made. All Geneva watches are sized by lines, a French measure equivalent to ·0888 of an inch; a watch size ten, that is ten lines in diameter, is therefore ·888 inches in diameter, say seven-eighths of an inch; one twenty-two size is ·1954, say two inches in diameter. The movements are sized in even number of lines, and the measurement is the diameter of the watch-plate. The case may be extended on the edge to make a movement appear bigger, but the size would be determined by the diameter of the pillar-plate, in the same way that English watches are sized. The thickness of a watch does not affect its size. A number showing the "lines" is generally punched on watch movements under the dial.

Slide-Rests.—These are used on lathes for the purpose of holding the tools firmly and guiding them definitely. They form a mechanical hand which has many points to recommend it instead of a human hand. The construction may be seen by reference to Figs. 93 and 94. The saddle slides along the bed, being actuated by a leading screw. In Fig. 93 there are three slides; the lower one is set to work at right angles to the line of centres, and the entire upper part of the rest swivels so that the middle and top slides can be put at any desired angle with the line of centres for turning conical. In Fig. 94 the angular motion is seen more clearly. The method of gripping the cutter is somewhat noticeable.

When using taper cutters remove the gib from under the

eccentric elevator and let it rest on the collar, not on the post, which can be screwed up or down to suit. Then by holding

Fig. 93. SLIDE-REST.

the cutter in position and turning the eccentric elevator, point of cutter can be brought to height desired. When using tools

Fig. 94. SLIDE-REST.

of square steel remove the eccentric elevator and replace the lower gib, by which the point of tool can be adjusted.

Sliding Tongs.—These have a pair of jaws which are held together by a link sliding on the handles. They are made tapering from the joint behind the jaws, so that when the link is close to the joint the jaws open to receive any

object to be held in them.   By sliding the link away from the
joint, the jaws are made to grip.   Sliding tongs are made
especially for some purposes, such as for holding hands whilst

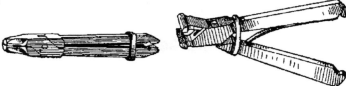

Figs 95, 96 SLIDING TONGS.

opening the holes to fit.   For most ordinary purposes to which
sliding tongs are applicable, a pin-vice serves equally well.

Slitting Files.—Small double-knife-edged or herring-bone
files, used for slitting heads of screws.

Split Seconds.—This is a form of hands used for timing
events of short duration, such as races, &c.   Two hands,
invariably centre seconds, revolve one immediately over the
other, and, on pressing a stop-piece, one hand is stopped, the
other continuing to revolve till stopped by a second pressure
on the push-piece ; the difference in the time as indicated by the
two hands shows the interval that has elapsed between the two
pressures on the stop-piece , a third pressure will set both
hands revolving again, which immediately on being released
resume their original position one over the other, appearing as
a single hand.

Sprung Over, or Under, refers to the position of the
balance-spring relative to the balance.   If sprung under,
the spring is below the balance and the index lies flat on the
plate of the movement ; when sprung above, the balance-spring
is over the balance and the index is fitted to the balance-cock.
All three-quarter-plate watches are sprung above.

Staff.—A plain arbor forming an axis, such as the balance
staff of a watch, which is a plain cylindrical piece of steel with
pivots formed at either end ; the axis of the lever and pallets

K

is also called a staff; when undistinguished by an adjective the balance-staff is usually understood to be meant.

Steady Pins.—These are the short pins, often two but sometimes three, which project from the bottom or foot of the several cocks and fit in holes in the plate, so that the cock is thereby held, so far as angular motion is concerned, independently of the screw which simply holds it firmly to the plate, and has nothing to do with steadying its position otherwise.

Stem Winder.—The usual form of keyless watches, which are wound from the pendant, through which a stem or arbor passes. (See "Keyless Mechanism" and "Pendant Winder.")

Stepping Appliance.—This is used on hollow mandrel lathes to form a step when using any slit-chuck. The long rod, Fig. 97, is passed through from the left end of the mandrel, the part marked A, being somewhat less in diameter than the work, slips inside the slit-chuck. The collar, B, steadies the rod inside the mandrel. The tapering bush, C, wedges in the tail end of the mandrel; and, by turning the milled head, D, the end, A, is placed at any required distance from the face of the chuck.

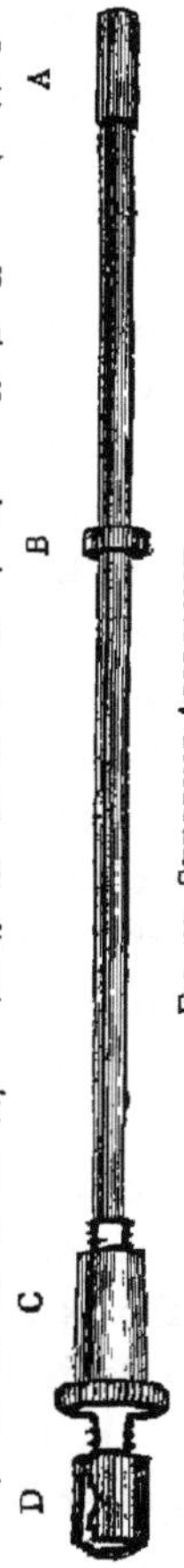

Stop-finger.—There are two distinct forms of stop-fingers; they form part of the stopwork, their use being to stop the action of the mainspring; in fusee watches the stop-finger is a jointed lever, which is raised by the winding of the chain to stop the fusee; it is sometimes called a chain-guard. In the going barrel the stop-finger gears with the Maltese cross. (See "Stopwork.")

Stop Watch.—One in which there is mechanism provided for stopping the hands. See ("Centre Seconds" and "Independent Seconds.")

Fig. 97. STEPPING APPLIANCE.

Stopwork.—This is an attachment to regulate the action of the mainspring, which stops the winding up when a certain point is reached, and prevents the spring from expending its entire force ; thus a more uniform power is obtained, the central part of the spring being used. Stopwork is especially necessary in watches having no fusee, to prevent the use of the highest and lowest powers of the spring, and in fusee watches to prevent overwinding. The stopwork used in each differs entirely in its construction , for going barrels the Maltese cross or Geneva stopwork is employed. This consists of a disc, having a single tooth or finger pinned on to the barrel arbor, and a star-wheel revolving on a stud in the barrel cover, having four spaces in which the single tooth acts ; when fully wound the finger butts against the solid periphery of the star-wheel ; as the barrel revolves the star-wheel is moved one tooth at each turn, and on completion of the fourth the finger again butts on the solid edge. Fusees have only to be stopped when fully wound, and a steel finger pivoted at one end is raised by the chain when making its last turn to catch a projecting snail on the fusee, and so prevent further winding.

Supplementary Arc.—Is that part of the vibration of the balance performed after the impulse has been given and due to the inertia of the balance itself, which is ultimately overcome by the force of the balance-spring, and the direction of motion is then changed.

Sunk Seconds.—The circle in which the seconds-hand travels is below the level of the dial in this kind of watch ; thus the liability of the hour- and seconds-hands catching and stopping the watch is reduced. The figures or divisions indicating seconds are painted on the sunk dial or on the edge of the main dial indifferently. The seconds dial is always a separate piece cemented into the main dial ; and in some cases the centre of the main dial is itself sunk to allow space for the

hour-hand, below the level of the circle on which the figures
are painted, so that it will be less liable to be caught by the
minute-hand.   Such a dial is said to have a sunk centre.

Swing-Rests.—These are very similar in their purpose to

Fig. 98. PLAIN SWING-REST.

slide-rests, but are constructed on quite another plan, as the
accompanying illustrations show.

Fig. 98 is a swing-rest, similar to the jewelling-rest shown
next, but it has no calliper.   It is very useful in cutting a
recess, and the cutters wings away from the work, to allow

Fig. 99. JEWELLING REST.

examination or the use of a hand-tool.   There are various
set-screws which govern the amount of motion given to the
cutter.

Fig. 99 is a swing-rest used for setting jewels. It may be made with callipers to measure the jewels and turn a recess to fit.

Fig. 100 shows a jewelling-rest, having a lateral screw and swing-calliper. As it registers and cuts recesses to correspond with various jewels, &c., that may be callipered, this rest is in constant use in watch factories. By arranging the cutter to be

Fig. 100. SWING-REST.

just midway between the joint on which the rest swings and the callipers, these move just twice the amount that the cutter does. By this plan holes are recessed to exactly fit whatever the jaws calliper.

Swing-wheel.—The name sometimes given to the escape-wheel driving a verge, in timepieces and watches.

Taps.—For cutting the threads in holes for screws, taps are used. Taps are used to cut threads on the interior, as screw-plates are used for the exterior thread. Machine-made screws, sold in packets, are generally accompanied by a piece of steel, specially prepared for making a tap. The threaded portion has to be filed to shape, hardened and tempered.

Third Wheel.—That one in the train coming next to the centre wheel, by which its pinion is driven.

Three-quarter-plate Watches.—The upper plate being cut away sufficiently to allow the balance and balance-cock to be placed on the pillar-plate, leaves about three-quarters of the entire circle ; hence the movement is called a three-quarter-plate. By placing the balance below the top-plate, the movement is made much thinner, and, generally with the same object, the cannon-pinion of a three-quarter-plate watch has no square projecting above the minute-hand, a hollow centre-pinion and set-hands-square being used instead. In a given diameter, the train of a three-quarter-plate must be much smaller than in a full-plate, so that unless flatness is a great consideration, the three-quarter-plate is not to be recommended, though its cost is greater.

Tempering.—This is the process of somewhat reducing the hardness of metals after hardening, and is chiefly a process in tool-making. Steel is tempered by heating, and the effect is made apparent by first cleaning a surface of the steel and observing the colour which comes upon it through oxidation when heated. The palest tinge of yellow appears first, and this deepens to orange, purple and blue if the heating is continued.

Timing-screws.—These are put in the rims of compensation balances to regulate the vibrations ; the screws have large, heavy heads, and by screwing them in towards the centre, the inertia of the balance is decreased, and *vice versâ*, but by removing a screw entirely the weight of the balance is correspondingly diminished, so that when, with all the screws screwed in to the fullest extent, the watch still loses, it is altered by removing some screws. In every case, when the timing-screws of a balance are moved, the greatest care must be exercised to keep the entire balance in equipoise. These screws are used principally in chronometers, where the length of the balance-spring must not be tampered with, as in using an ordinary regulator with curb-pins confining the action of the balance-spring. The positions of the screws on the arms of the balance are arranged to produce an alteration in the inertia corresponding with the alteration in the spring; but the timing-screws are usually tapped in the rim at the point immediately contiguous to the cross-bar

Timing-stand.—Used to hold a watch movement in any desired position so that it may be adjusted to perform equally in any position.

Train.—The whole of the wheel-work by which the power of the mainspring is transmitted to the escape-wheel; it comprises the centre, third and fourth wheels, and all their pinions, and also the escape-pinion.

Turns.—This is the lathe of the watch repairer, and sometimes called a turn-bench. The form of the tool is modified

Fig 101.
TIMING-STAND.

in various localities, but it has always dead or fixed centres. The Continental form is a steel bar having one sliding poppit, and the other poppit solid with the bar-bed. A small T-rest, having motion along the bed and at right angles to it, also forms part of this tool. The centres are usually round, and are fixed by plain thumb-clamping screws. The ends of these centres are shaped to suit various purposes for which the turns are employed. The work to be turned is provided with a ferrule, and mounted between the centres.

Tweezers.—These tools are invariably used for handling all kinds of small watchwork, and are made of two blades, generally of steel, riveted together at one end and shaped to a point at the other. The points spring open about one-quarter to one-half of an inch, and any small object may be grasped between the points by pressing the tweezers together with the thumb and finger. Tweezers are usually about four inches long, and may be made of any shape. Sometimes they are made of brass, so as not to damage work by scratching.

Uprighting Tool.—Used for marking the position of pivot-

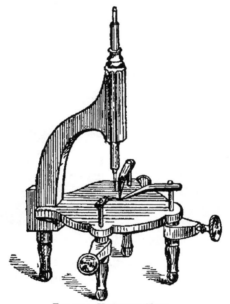

Fig. 102. UPRIGHT TOOL.

holes and ensuring that they are precisely upright. The tool consists of a circular base-plate mounted on three feet, and having an arm from the edge of the plate supporting a cannon immediately above the centre. Beneath the plate another cannon is also fixed. The holes through these two cannons must be perfectly straight with each other, and also perfectly at right angles to the surface of the base plate. Pointed rods, accurately fitting the cannon boring, are used. The watch movement is laid upon the base-plate with the lower hole upon the point of the rod in the cannon. The top rod is then brought down, and it marks a spot precisely upright to the lower hole. If a hole be drilled through this spot it will be upright to the lower hole.

Verge Stake.—A piece of steel, usually fitted in a block of brass, having a hole and a radial slit to allow the free passage of a verge ; thus forming a stake for the verge collet to rest on when riveting the balance or otherwise treating it.

Wheel Cutting. — This is the process of making

Figs. 103, 104. WHEEL-CUTTERS.

the spaces between the teeth of wheels. Wheel-cutting engines are machines specially made for the purpose, and are generally used in making large numbers of wheels. Some apparatus for use on the lathe are shown below. They go on the slide-rest and are driven by a band from the counter shaft. The cutter can be run either way by twisting the band to suit. The work, blank wheels or pinions, is held on the lathe centres or in a chuck. Fig. 103 shows the most simple style of wheel-cutting apparatus, it having only one spindle.

Fig. 104 shows a wheel and pinion-cutter, with three spindles.

Each spindle, with its cutter, has separate adjustments, and is held in position by a pawle.

Fig. 105 is a wheel-cutting arrangement attached to the lower plate of a slide-rest. It is designed for cutting all kinds of wheels and pinions used in watchwork.

Fig. 105. WHEEL-CUTTER.

Wheel-cutting Engine.—The machine used for cutting the wheel-teeth in watches. It consists of an apparatus for holding the wheel blanks firmly, and which also allows them to be revolved and fixed at certain points according to the number of teeth. The cutter for cutting the teeth, or rather the spaces between them, is revolved rapidly and brought across the periphery of the blank at right angles to the wheel. Thus one space is cut. The blank is then rotated an aliquot part of the distance to give the necessary number of teeth, and a cut is made, these operations being repeated till the entire periphery of the wheel-blank is furnished with teeth

Wheel Stretcher.—A tool specially contrived for stretching wheels, that is, enlarging them by extending the outer rim. This is effected by hammering the wheel equally all round its circumference. Frequently this is done with an ordinary hammer on a plain stake, but the wheel-stretching tool is designed to act with greater certainty. When a depth is shallow, it is sometimes corrected by stretching the wheel; but, obviously, the practice is not to be commended.

Wig-wag.—This is the name given by our American

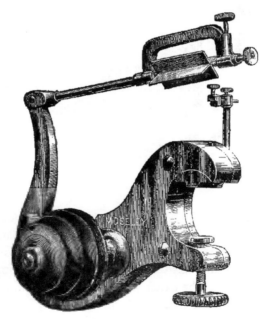

Fig. 106. Wig-wag.

cousins to the appliance illustrated by Fig. 106. It is used for polishing staffs, pivots, and shoulders of pinions, pinion-leaves, &c. It is chiefly used in watch factories.

Wire.—The bright steel wire commonly used in watch-work is sold in lengths of one foot each. The sizes are measured by a special plate-gauge having a range of sixty holes; the following shows the diameters of the wire in thousandths of an inch equivalent to the sixty sizes.

1 = ·228	21 = ·159	41 = ·096
2 = ·221	22 = ·157	42 = ·093
3 = ·213	23 = ·154	43 = ·089
4 — ·209	24 = ·152	44 = ·086
5 = ·205	25 = ·149	45 = ·082
6 = ·204	26 = ·147	46 = ·081
7 = ·201	27 = ·144	47 = ·078
8 = ·199	28 = ·140	48 = ·076
9 = ·196	29 = ·136	49 = ·073
10 = ·193	30 = ·128	50 = ·070
11 = ·191	31 = ·120	51 = ·067
12 = ·189	32 = ·116	52 = ·063
13 = ·185	33 = ·113	53 = ·059
14 = ·182	34 = ·111	54 = ·055
15 = ·180	35 = ·110	55 = ·052
16 = ·177	36 = ·106	56 = ·046
17 = 173	37 = ·104	57 = ·043
18 = ·169	38 = ·101	58 = ·042
19 = ·166	39 = ·099	59 = ·041
20 = ·161	40 = ·098	60 = ·040

INDEX.

STATIONERS' HALL COURT, LONDON, E C.
January, 1887

STANDARD BOOKS

IN

ENGINEERING, MECHANICS, BUILDING,

THE INDUSTRIAL ARTS, MANUFACTURES,

ETC ETC.

PUBLISHED BY

CROSBY LOCKWOOD & CO.

CIVIL ENGINEERING, SURVEYING, &c.

The Water Supply of Cities and Towns.

A COMPREHENSIVE TREATISE on the WATER-SUPPLY OF CITIES AND TOWNS By WILLIAM HUMBER, A M Inst C.E , and M Inst M E , Author of "Cast and Wrought Iron Bridge Construction," &c , &c. Illustrated with 50 Double Plates, 1 Single Plate, Coloured Frontispiece, and upwards of 250 Woodcuts, and containing 400 pages of Text Imp 4to, £6 6s. elegantly and substantially half-bound in morocco

" The most systematic and valuable work upon water supply hitherto produced in English, or in any other language Mr Humber's work is characterised almost throughout by an exhaustiveness much more distinctive of French and German than of English technical treatises "—*Engineer*

"We can congratulate Mr Humber on having been able to give so large an amount of information on a subject so important as the water supply of cities and towns The plates fifty in number, are mostly drawings of executed works, and alone would have commanded the attention of every engineer whose practice may be in this branch of the profession —*Builder*

Cast and Wrought Iron Bridge Construction.

A COMPLETE AND PRACTICAL TREATISE ON CAST AND WROUGHT IRON BRIDGE CONSTRUCTION, including Iron Foundations. In Three Parts—Theoretical, Practical, and Descriptive. By WILLIAM HUMBER, A M Inst C E , and M Inst M E Third Edition revised and much improved, with 115 Double Plates. In Two Vols imp, 4to, £6 16s 6d half-bound in morocco

" Mr Humber's stately volumes, lately issued—in which the most important bridges erected during the last five years under the direction of the late Mr Brunel, Sir W Cubitt, Mr Hawkshaw, Mr Page Mr Fowler Mr Hemans, and others among our most eminent engineers, are drawn and specified in great detail —*Engineer*

Oblique Bridges.

A PRACTICAL AND THEORETICAL ESSAY ON OBLIQUE BRIDGES With 13 large Plates By the late GEORGE WATSON BUCK, M.I.C.E. Third Edition, revised by his Son, J. H WATSON BUCK, M I C E , and with the addition of Description to Diagrams for facilitating the Construction of Oblique Bridges by W. H. BARLOW, M.I C E Royal 8vo. 12s cloth.

" The standard text-book for all engineers regarding skew arches, is Mr Buck's treatise and it would be impossible to consult a better ' —*Engineer*

B

Bridge Construction in Masonry, Timber & Iron.

*EXAMPLES OF BRIDGE AND VIADUCT CONSTRUC-
TION OF MASONRY, TIMBER AND IRON* Consisting of 46 Plates
from the Contract Drawings or Admeasurement of select Works   By
W. D HASKOLL, C E   Second Edition, with the Addition of 554 Estimates, and the Practice of Setting out Works. Illustrated with 6 pages
of Diagrams. Imp. 4to, £2 12s 6d half-morocco.

"A work of the present nature by a man of Mr Haskoll's experience must prove invaluable The tables of estimates will considerably enhance its value '—*Engineering*

Earthwork.

EARTHWORK TABLES. Showing the Contents in Cubic
Yards of Embankments, Cuttings, &c., of Heights or Depths up to an
average of 80 feet. By JOSEPH BROADBENT, C E , and FRANCIS CAMPIN,
C E. Crown 8vo, 5s cloth.

"The way in which accuracy is attained, by a simple division of each cross section into
three elements, two in which are constant and one variable, is ingenious '—*Athenæum*

Barlow's Strength of Materials, enlarged.

A TREATISE ON THE STRENGTH OF MATERIALS ,
with Rules for Application in Architecture, the Construction of Suspen-
sion Bridges, Railways, &c. By PETER BARLOW, F.R S. Arranged and
Edited by W. HUMBER, A.M Inst C E. Demy 8vo, 400 pp., with 19 large
Plates and numerous Woodcuts. 18s. cloth.

"Valuable alike to the student, tyro, and the experienced practitioner, it will always rank
in future as it has hitherto done, as the standard treatise on that particular subject '—
Engineer

"A book which no engineer of any kind can afford to be without "—*Colliery Guardian*
"There is no greater authority than Barlow —*Building News*

Survey Practice.

*AID TO SURVEY PRACTICE, for Reference in Surveying,
Levelling, Setting-out and in Route Surveys of Travellers by Land and Sea*
With Tables, Illustrations, and Records.   By LOWIS D'A JACKSON,
A.M.I.C.E., Author of "Hydraulic Manual," "Modern Metrology," &c.
Large crown 8vo, 12s. 6d. cloth.

"Mr Jackson has produced a valuable *vade mecum* for the surveyor We can recommend
this book as containing an admirable supplement to the teaching of the accomplished surveyor "—*Athenæum*

"The author brings to his work a fortunate union of theory and practical experience,
which, aided by a clear and lucid style of writing, renders the book a very useful one "—
Builder.

Levelling.

*A TREATISE ON THE PRINCIPLES AND PRACTICE
OF LEVELLING* By FREDERICK W. SIMMS, F G.S , M I C.E. Seventh
Edition, with the Addition of LAW's "Practical Examples for Setting-out
Railway Curves," and TRAUTWINE's "Field Practice of Laying-out Cir-
cular Curves " With 7 Plates and numerous Woodcuts, 8vo, 8s, 6d. cloth.

*** TRAUTWINE on Curves, separate, 5s.

" I! e text book on levelling in most of our engineering schools and colleges "—*Engineer.*
"The publishers have rendered a substantial service to the profession, especially to the
younger members, by bringing out the present edition of Mr Simms' useful work "—
Engineering.

Tunnelling.

PRACTICAL TUNNELLING. By FREDERICK W. SIMMS,
F.G.S., M. Inst C E. Third Edition, Revised and Extended by D. KIN
NEAR CLARK, M.Inst.C E Imp. 8vo, with 21 Folding Plates and numerous
Wood Engravings. 30s cloth.

"It has been regarded from th. first as a text book of the subject .   . Mr. Clark has
added immensely to the value of the book "—*Engineer*
"The additional chapters by Mr Clark, containing as they do numerous examples of
modern practice, bring the book well up to date "—*Engineering*

Statics, Graphic and Analytic.

GRAPHIC AND ANALYTIC STATICS, in Theory and Comparison Their Practical Application to the Treatment of Stresses in Roofs and other Frameworks. To which is added a Chapter on Wind Pressures By R. HUDSON GRAHAM, C E. With numerous Examples, many taken from existing Structures. Second Edition, Revised and Enlarged 8vo, 16s. cloth.

"Mr Graham's book will find a place wherever graphic and analytic statics are used or studied '—*Engineer*

'The work is excellent from a practical point of view, and has evidently been prepared with much care The directions for working are ample, and are illustrated by an abundance of well selected examples It is an excellent text-book for the practical draughtsman"—*Athenæum*

Strains, Formulæ & Diagrams for Calculation of.

A HANDY BOOK for the CALCULATION OF STRAINS IN GIRDERS AND SIMILAR STRUCTURES, AND THEIR STRENGTH By WILLIAM HUMBER, A M I C E, &c Fourth Edition Crown 8vo, nearly 100 Woodcuts and 3 Plates, 7s. 6d cloth.

"The formulæ are neatly expressed, and the diagrams good '—*Athenæum*

"We heartily commend this really *handy* book to our engineer and architect readers '—*English Mechanic*

Hydraulic Tables.

HYDRAULIC TABLES, CO-EFFICIENTS, AND FORMULÆ for Finding the Discharge of Water from Orifices, Notches, Weirs, Pipes, and Rivers. With New Formulæ, Tables and General Information on Rainfall, Catchment-Basins, Drainage, Sewerage, Water Supply for Towns, and Mill Power. By JOHN NEVILLE, Civil Engineer, M R I A Third Edition, carefully revised, with considerable Additions. Numerous Illustrations Crown 8vo, 14s. cloth.

"It is, of all English books on the subject, the one nearest to completion . . From the good arrangement of the matter, the clear explanations, and abundance of formulæ, the carefully-calculated tables, and, above all, the thorough acquaintance with both theory and construction which is displayed from first to last, the book will be found to be an acquisition —*Architect*

Hydraulics.

HYDRAULIC MANUAL Consisting of Working Tables and Explanatory Text Intended as a Guide in Hydraulic Calculations and Field Operations By LOWIS D'A JACKSON. Fourth Edition. Rewritten and Enlarged. Large crown 8vo, 16s. cloth.

"From the great mass of material at his command the author has constructed a manual which may be accepted as a trustworthy guide to this branch of the engineer's profession We can heartily recommend this volume to all who desire to be acquainted with the latest development of this important subject —*Engineering*

Tramways and their Working.

TRAMWAYS THEIR CONSTRUCTION AND WORKING Embracing a Comprehensive History of the System, with an exhaustive Analysis of the various Modes of Traction, a Description of the Varieties of Rolling Stock, and ample Details of Cost and Working Expenses. By D KINNEAR CLARK, M Inst C E With over 200 Wood Engravings, and 13 Folding Plates. Two Vols, large crown 8vo, 30s cloth.

"All interested in tramways must refer to it, as all railway engineers have turned to the author's work 'Railway Machinery.'"—*Engineer*

"The best form of rails, the best mode of construction, and the best mechanical appliances are so fairly indicated in the work under review, that any engineer about to construct a tramway will be enabled at once to obtain the practical information which will be of most service to him "—*Athenæum*.

Tables for Setting-out Curves.

TABLES OF TANGENTIAL ANGLES AND MULTI-PLES for Setting-out Curves from 5 to 200 Radius By ALEXANDER BEAZELEY, M Inst C E. Third Edition   Printed on 48 Cards, and sold in a cloth box, waistcoat-pocket size, 3s 6d.

" Each table is printed on a small card, which, being placed on the Theodolite, leaves the hands free to manipulate the instrument—no small advantage as regards the rapidity of work."
Engineer

Engineering Fieldwork.

THE PRACTICE OF ENGINEERING FIELDWORK, applied to Land and Hydraulic, Hydrographic, and Submarine Surveying and Levelling   Second Edition, Revised, with considerable Additions, and a Supplement on Waterworks, Sewers, Sewage, and Irrigation   By W DAVIS HASKOLL. C.E.   Numerous Folding Plates   In One Volume, demy 8vo, £1 5s cloth

Large Tunnel Shafts.

*THE CONSTRUCTION OF LARGE TUNNEL SHAFTS ·
A Practical and Theoretical Essay*   By J H WATSON BUCK, M Inst C E, Resident Engineer, London and North-Western Railway.   Illustrated with Folding plates   Royal 8vo, 12s cloth

" Will be regarded by civil engineers as of the utmost value, and calculated to save much time and obviate many mistakes "—*Colliery Guardian*

Surveying.

LAND AND MARINE SURVEYING, in reference to the Preparation of Plans for Roads and Railways, Canals, Rivers, Towns' Water Supplies, Docks and Harbours, with Description and Use of Surveying Instruments   By W DAVIS HASKOLL   Second Edition, revised with Additions   Large crown 8vo, with 13 Plates, 9s. cloth
[Just Published.

Field-Book for Engineers.

THE ENGINEER'S, MINING SURVEYOR'S, and CON-TRACTOR'S FIELD-BOOK   Consisting of a Series of Tables, with Rules, Explanations of Systems and use of Theodolite for Traverse Surveying and Plotting the Work with minute accuracy by means of Straight Edge and Set Square only, Levelling with the Theodolite. Setting-out Curves without Theodolite, &c, &c   By W DAVIS HASKOLL, C E   With numerous Woodcuts.   Fourth Edition, Enlarged.   Crown 8vo, 12s. cloth.

The book is very handy, and the author might have added that the separate tables of sines and tangents to every minute would make it useful for many other purposes, the genuine traverse tables existing all the same   —*Athenæum*

Earthwork, Measurement and Calculation of.

A MANUAL ON EARTHWORK. By ALEX J. S GRAHAM, C E   With numerous Diagrams.   18mo, 2s. 6d. cloth,

Strains.

THE STRAINS ON STRUCTURES OF IRONWORK, with Practical Remarks on Iron Construction   By F W SHEILDS, M Inst. C E   Second Edition, with 5 Plates.   Royal 8vo, 5s. cloth.
" The student cannot find a better book on this subject "—*Engineer*

Strength of Cast Iron, etc.

A PRACTICAL ESSAY ON THE STRENGTH of CAST IRON AND OTHER METALS   By THOMAS TREDGOLD, C E.   Fifth Edition, including HODGKINSON'S Experimental Researches.   8vo, 12s. cloth.

MECHANICS AND MECHANICAL ENGINEERING.

Mechanic's Workshop Companion.

THE PRACTICAL MECHANIC'S WORKSHOP COM-PANION Comprising a great variety of the most useful Rules and Formulæ in Mechanical Science, with numerous Tables of Practical Data and Calculated Results for facilitating Mechanical Operations By W Templeton, Author of "The Engineer's Practical Assistant" An Entirely New Edition, Revised, Modernised and considerably Enlarged by Walter S. Hutton, C.E. With upwards of 250 Illustrations. Fcap, 6s leather [*Just published.*

" It has met with great success in the engineering workshop, as we can testify, and there are a great many men who, in a great measure, owe their rise in life to this little book "—*Building News*

Engineer's and Machinist's Assistant.

The ENGINEER'S, MILLWRIGHT'S, and MACHINIST'S PRACTICAL ASSISTANT Comprising a collection of Useful Tables, Rules and Data Compiled and Arranged, with Original Matter, by William Templeton Seventh Edition. Carefully Revised, with Additions 18mo, 2s 6d. cloth

'A more suitable present to an apprentice to any of the mechanical trades could not possibly be made —*Building News*

Mechanics.

THE HANDBOOK OF MECHANICS By Dionysius Lardner, D C L, formerly Professor of Natural Philosophy and Astronomy in University College, London New Edition, Edited and considerably Enlarged by Benjamin Loewy, F R A S, &c 378 Illustrations, post 8vo, 6s cloth

" The explanations throughout are studiously popular, and care has been taken to show the application of the various branches of physics to the industrial arts, and to the practical business of life —*Mining Journal*

Turning.

LATHE-WORK · A Practical Treatise on the Tools, Appliances, and Processes employed in the Art of Turning. By Paul N. Hasluck. Third Edition, Revised and Enlarged Crown 8vo, 5s cloth.

[*Just published.*

" Written by a man who knows, not only how work ought to be done, but who also knows how to do it, and how to convey his knowledge to others To all turners this book would be valuable —*Engineering*

Iron and Steel.

IRON AND STEEL A Work for the Forge, Foundry, Factory, and Office. Containing ready, useful, and trustworthy Information for Ironmasters and their Stock-takers, Managers of Bar, Rail, Plate, and Sheet Rolling Mills, Iron and Metal Founders, Mechanical, Mining, and Consulting Engineers, &c &c By Chas Hoare Eighth Edition, Revised and Enlarged Oblong 32mo, leather, elastic band, 6s

" For comprehensiveness the book has not its equal "—*Iron*

" One of the best of the pocket books, and a useful companion in other branches of work than iron and steel '—*English Mechanic*

Stone-working Machinery.

STONE-WORKING MACHINERY, and the Rapid and Economical Conversion of Stone With Hints on the Arrangement and Management of Stone Works. By M Powis Bale, M I M E, A M.I.C E. With numerous Illustrations. Large crown 8vo, 9s cloth.

" The book should be in the hands of every mason or student of stone-work "—*Colliery Guardian*

Engineer's Reference Book.

THE WORKS' MANAGER'S HANDBOOK OF MODERN RULES, TABLES, AND DATA For Engineers, Millwrights, Boiler Makers; Tool Makers, Machinists, and Metal Workers, Iron and Brass Founders, &c. By W. S. HUTTON, Civil and Mechanical Engineer Third Edition, carefully Revised, with Additions. In One handsome Volume, medium 8vo, price 15s, strongly bound.   [*Just published*

Contents ·

Proportions and Rules for Modern Stationary and Locomotive Engines—Lancashire, Cornish, Vertical, Return Tube, and Portable Engine Boilers—Chimneys—Water Wheels, Pumps, Pipes, Girders, Gearing, Shafting, and Millwork—Iron Foundry Work and Brass Work—Rules and Practical Data relating to the Strength and Weight of Metals and Materials—Iron and Brass Casting—Cutting Metals—Wheel Cutting—Screw Cutting—Wheel Gearing—Rope Gearing—Pulleys—Weight of Pulleys—Weight of Spur,

Bevel, and Mortice Wheels—Warming and Ventilating—Weight of Iron, Steel, Brass, and various Metals and Materials

Also, The Indicator and Indicator Diagrams. Various Memoranda for the Foundry and Workshop—Rules for the Weight of Castings—The New Patent Law and Costs of Patents—Legal Memoranda—List of French Words for English Engineering Terms—French and English Weights and Measures—And a variety of Modern Practical Information for Civil and Mechanical Engineers

"The volume is an exceedingly useful one, brimful with engineers' notes, memoranda, and rules, and well worthy of being on every mechanical engineer's bookshelf   . There is valuable information on every page "—*Mechanical World*

"The information is precisely that likely to be required in practice . The work forms a desirable addition to the library, not only of the works' manager, but of anyone connected with general engineering "—*Mining Journal*

"A formidable mass of facts and figures, readily accessible through an elaborate index Such a volume will be found absolutely necessary as a book of reference in all sort of 'works' connected with the metal trades Any ordinary foreman or workman can find all he wants in the crowded pages of this useful work '—*Ryland's Iron Trades Circular*

Engineering Construction.

PATTERN-MAKING · A Practical Treatise, embracing the Main Types of Engineering Construction, together with the methods of Estimating the Weight of Castings; to which is added an Appendix of Tables for Workshop Reference By a FOREMAN PATTERN MAKER. With upwards of Three Hundred and Seventy Illustrations. Crown 8vo, 7s. 6d cloth.   [*Just published.*

"A well written technical guide, evidently written by a man who understands and has practised what he has written about, he says what he has to say in a plain, straightforward manner We cordially recommend the treatise to engineering students, young journeymen, and others desirous of being initiated into the mysteries of pattern-making "—*Builder*

Smith's Tables for Mechanics. etc.

TABLES, MEMORANDA, and CALCULATED RESULTS, FOR MECHANICS, ENGINEERS, ARCHITECTS, BUILDERS, &c. Selected and Arranged by FRANCIS SMITH. Third Edition, Revised and Enlarged, 250 pp, waistcoat pocket size, 1s. 6d. limp leather

[*Just published.*

"It would, perhaps, be as difficult to make a small pocket book selection of notes and formulæ to suit ALL engineers as it would be to make a universal medicine, but Mr Smith's waistcoat-pocket collection may be looked upon as a successful attempt "—*Engineer.*

"A veritable pocket treasury of knowledge '—*Iron.*

Railway Working.

SAFE RAILWAY WORKING. A Treatise on Railway Accidents. Their Cause and Prevention. With a Description of Modern Appliances and Systems. By CLEMENT E STRETTON, C E, Vice-President and Consulting Engineer of the Amalgamated Society of Railway Servants. Crown 8vo, 4s 6d cloth   [*Just published*

"A very useful and instructive book, and one that will assist in bringing before interested people the requirements that are necessary for the safe working of railways."—*Mechanical World.*

Chain Cables.

CHAIN CABLES AND CHAINS Comprising Sizes and Curves of Links, Studs, &c., Iron for Cables and Chains, Chain Cable and Chain Making, Forming and Welding Links, Strength of Cables and Chains, Certificates for Cables, Marking Cables, Prices of Chain Cables and Chains, Historical Notes, Acts of Parliament, Statutory Tests, Charges for Testing, List of Manufacturers of Cables, &c , &c. With numerous Tables, Illustrations and Lithographic Drawings. By THOMAS W TRAILL, C E , R N   Folio, £2 2s. cloth, bevelled boards

' Nothing seems to be wanting to make it a complete, handsome and standard work of reference on the subject of chain cables and chains "—*Nautical Magazine.*

Steam Boilers.

A TREATISE ON STEAM BOILERS · Their Strength, Construction, and Economical Working. By ROBERT WILSON C.E.   Fifth Edition. 12mo, 6s. cloth

' The best treatise that has ever been published on steam boilers."—*Engineer*

" The author shows himself perfect master of his subject, and we heartily recommend all employing steam power to possess themselves of the work '—*Ryland's Iron Trades Circular*

Boiler Making.

THE BOILER-MAKER'S READY RECKONER. With Examples of Practical Geometry and Templating, for the Use of Platers, Smiths and Riveters. By JOHN COURTNEY. Edited by D. K. CLARK, M I C E. Second Edition, with Additions 12mo, 5s. half-bound.

A reliable guide to the working boiler-maker "—*Iron*

" Boiler-makers will readily recognise the value of this volume The tables are clearly printed, and so arranged that they can be referred to with the greatest facility, so that they will be generally appreciated and much used "—*Mining Journal.*

Steam Engine.

TEXT-BOOK ON THE STEAM ENGINE : With a Supplement on GAS ENGINES By T M GOODEVE, M A , Barrister at-Law, Author of " The Elements of Mechanism," &c. Eighth Edition, Enlarged. Crown 8vo, 6s cloth.

' Professor Goodeve has given us a treatise which will bear comparison with anything written by Huxley or Maxwell, and we can award it no higher praise —*Engineer*

Portable Engine.

THE PORTABLE ENGINE · Its Construction and Management. A Practical Manual for Owners and Users of Steam Engines generally. By W. D. WANSBROUGH. Crown 8vo, 3s. 6d cloth

[*Just published.*

"A very complete manual for users in the construction and management of steam engines '—*Building News.*

Steam.

THE SAFE USE OF STEAM Containing Rules for Unprofessional Steam-users. By an ENGINEER Fifth Edition. Sewed, 6d.

' If steam-users would but learn this little book by heart, boiler explosions would become sensations by their rarity —*English Mechanic*

Coal and Speed Tables.

A POCKET BOOK OF COAL AND SPEED TABLES, for Engineers and Steam-users. By NELSON FOLEY, Author of " Boiler Construction " Pocket-size, 3s 6d. cloth , 4s. leather.

Gas Lighting.

COMMON SENSE FOR GAS-USERS A Catechism of Gas-Lighting for Householders, Gasfitters, Millowners, Architects, Engineers, etc By ROBERT WILSON, C E., Author of " A Treatise on Steam Boilers." Second Edition. Crown 8vo, sewed, with Folding Plates, 2s 6d.

THE POPULAR WORKS OF MICHAEL REYNOLDS

(*Known as* "The Engine Driver's Friend")

Locomotive-Engine Driving.

LOCOMOTIVE-ENGINE DRIVING : *A Practical Manual for Engineers in charge of Locomotive Engines* By Michael Reynolds, M S E , formerly Locomotive Inspector L B. and S C R Seventh Edition Including a Key to the Locomotive Engine With Illustrations and Portrait of the Author Crown 8vo, 4s 6d. cloth.

"Mr Reynolds has supplied a want, and has supplied it well We can confidently recommend the book, not only to the practical driver, but to everyone who takes an interest in the performance of locomotive engines - *The Engineer*

"Mr Reynolds has opened a new chapter in the literature of the day Of the practical utility of Mr Reynolds's book we have to speak in terms of warm commendation '— *Athenæum*

The Engineer, Fireman, and Engine-Boy.

THE MODEL LOCOMOTIVE ENGINEER, FIREMAN, *and ENGINE-BOY* Comprising a Historical Notice of the Pioneer Locomotive Engines and their Inventors, with a project for the establishment of Certificates of Qualification in the Running Service of Railways By Michael Reynolds, M S.E. With numerous Illustrations and a fine Portrait of George Stephenson. Crown 8vo, 4s 6d cloth

"From the technical knowledge of the author it will appeal to the railway man of to-day more forcibly than anything written by Dr Smiles The volume contains information of a technical kind, and facts that every driver should be familiar with "—*English Mechanic*

Stationary Engine Driving.

STATIONARY ENGINE DRIVING A Practical Manual *for Engineers in Charge of Stationary Engines* By M Reynolds Third Edition, Enlarged With Plates and Woodcuts Cr 8vo, 4s. 6d cloth

"The author is thoroughly acquainted with his subjects, and his advice on the various points treated is clear and practical He has produced a manual which is an exceedingly useful one for the class for whom it is specially intended '—*Engineering*

"Our author leaves no stone unturned He is determined that his readers shall not only know something about the stationary engine, but all about it '—*Engineer*

Continuous Railway Brakes.

CONTINUOUS RAILWAY BRAKES A Practical Treatise *on the several Systems in Use in the United Kingdom* , their Construction and Performance With copious Illustrations and numerous Tables. By Michael Reynolds Large crown 8vo, 9s, cloth

' May be recommended to all who desire to study the subject of continuous brakes — *Iron*

Engine-Driving Life.

ENGINE-DRIVING LIFE , *or, Stirring Adventures and Incidents in the Lives of Locomotive-Engine Drivers.* By Michael Reynolds Ninth Thousand Crown 8vo, 2s cloth

The book from first to last is perfectly fascinating Wilkie Collins's most thrilling conceptions are thrown into the shade by true incidents, endless in their variety, related in every page '—*North British Mail*

"Anyone who wishes to get a real insight into railway life cannot do better than read 'Engine-Driving Life ' for himself, and if he once take it up he will find that the author's enthusiasm and real love of the engine driving profession will carry him on till he has read every page '—*Saturday Review*

Pocket Companion for Enginemen.

THE ENGINEMAN'S POCKET COMPANION, AND PRACTICAL EDUCATOR FOR ENGINEMEN, BOILER ATTENDANTS AND MECHANICS By Michael Reynolds, Mem S E , Author of "Locomotive Engine-Driving," "Stationary Engine-Driving," &c With Forty-five Illustrations and numerous Diagrams. Royal 18mo, 3s. 6d., strongly bound in cloth for pocket wear   [*Just published*

ARCHITECTURE, BUILDING, etc.

Construction.

THE SCIENCE OF BUILDING An Elementary Treatise on *the Principles of Construction* By E WYNDHAM TARN, M A , Architect. Second Edition, Revised, with 58 Engravings. Crown 8vo, 7s 6d cloth

" very valuable book, which we strongly recommend to all students "—*Builder*

"No architectural student should be without this handbook of constructional knowledge —*Architect*

Useful Text-Book for Architects.

THE ARCHITECT'S GUIDE Being a Text-Book of Useful *Information for Architects, Engineers, Surveyors, Contractors Clerks of Works, &c , &c.* By FREDERICK ROGERS, Architect Second Edition, Revised and Enlarged With numerous Illustrations Crown 8vo, 6s. cloth.

"As a text book of useful information for architects engineers, surveyors, &c , it would be hard to find a handier or more complete little volume '—*Standard*

"A young architect could hardly have a better guide book '—*Timber Trades Journal.*

Drawing for Builders and Students in Architecture.

PRACTICAL RULES ON DRAWING, *for the Operative Builder and Young Student in Architecture.* By GEORGE PYNE With 14 Plates. 4to, 7s. 6d. boards.

The House-Owner's Estimator.

THE HOUSE-OWNER'S ESTIMATOR , or, What will it Cost to Build, Alter, or Repair ? A Price Book adapted to the Use of Unprofessional People, as well as for the Architectural Surveyor and Builder By the late JAMES D SIMON, A R I B A. Edited and Revised by FRANCIS T W MILLER, A R I B A With numerous Illustrations Third Edition, Revised Crown 8vo 3s 6d. cloth

"In two years it will repay its cost a hundred times over '—*Field*

"A very handy book "—*English Mechanic*

Designing, Measuring, and Valuing.

THE STUDENT'S GUIDE to the PRACTICE of MEASUR-*ING AND VALUING ARTIFICERS' WORKS* Containing Directions for taking Dimensions, Abstracting the same, and bringing the Quantities into Bill, with Tables of Constants, and Copious Memoranda for the Valuation of Labour and Materials With 8 Plates and 63 Woodcuts Originally edited by EDWARD DOBSON, Architect Fifth Edition, Revised, with considerable Additions, by E. WYNDHAM TARN, M A Crown 8vo, 9s cloth.

"Well fulfils the promise of its title-page, and we can thoroughly recommend it to the class for whose use it has been compiled Mr Tarn's additions and revisions have much increased the usefulness of the work, and have especially augmented its value to students. —*Engineering*

"This edition will be found the most complete treatise on the principles of measuring and valuing artificers work that has yet been published —*Building News*

Handbook of Specifications.

THE HANDBOOK OF SPECIFICATIONS. By Professor T. L. DONALDSON, late P R I.B.A , &c New Edition. In One large Vol , 8vo, with upwards of 1,000 pages of Text, and 33 Plates. £1 11s 6d. cloth.

Pocket Estimator.

THE POCKET ESTIMATOR for the BUILDING TRADES. By A C Beaton. Third Edition, carefully revised, 33 Woodcuts, leather waistcoat-pocket size, 1s 6d.

" Contains a good deal of information not easily to be obtained from the ordinary price books The prices given are accurate, and up to date."—*Building News*

Builder's & Surveyor's Pocket Technical Guide.

THE POCKET TECHNICAL GUIDE AND MEAS-URER FOR BUILDERS AND SURVEYORS. By A C Beaton. Second Edition, with 19 Woodcuts, leather, waistcoat-pocket size, 1s 6d

" An exceedingly handy pocket companion, thoroughly reliable "—*Builder's Weekly Reporter.*

Bricks and Tiles.

THE PRACTICAL BRICK AND TILE BOOK. Comprising I A Rudimentary Treatise on Brick and Tile Making, by Edward Dobson, A I.C.E., M.I B.A. II. The Rudiments of Practical Bricklaying, by Adam Hammond III. Brickwork A Practical Treatise on Bricklaying, Cutting and Setting, by F. Walker. 12mo, 6s. strongly half-bound. [*Just Published.*

CARPENTRY, TIMBER, etc.

Tredgold's Carpentry, Enlarged by E. W. Tarn.

THE ELEMENTARY PRINCIPLES OF CARPENTRY. A Treatise on the Pressure and Equilibrium of Timber Framing, the Resistance of Timber, and the Construction of Floors, Arches, Bridges, Roofs, Uniting Iron and Stone with Timber, &c. With numerous Tables of the Scantlings of Timber for different purposes, the Specific Gravities of Materials, &c. By Thomas Tredgold, C E. Seventh Edition, thoroughly Revised and considerably Enlarged by E. Wyndham Tarn, M A. With 61 Plates, Portrait of the Author, and several Woodcuts. In one large Vol , 4to, price £1 5s cloth. [*Just published.*

" Ought to be in every architect's and every builder's library."—*Builder*

" Tredgold's 'Elementary Principles of Carpentry' is without doubt, the standard English authority upon the subject Mr Tarn, by supplementing the text of the author, adds much to the work, and makes it an indispensable addition to the library of the student, the architect, and the engineer '—*Building News*

Woodworking Machinery.

WOODWORKING MACHINERY: Its Rise, Progress, and Construction. Illustrated with Examples of Recent Designs by leading English, French, and American Engineers. By M Powis Bale, A M Inst C.E , M I M.E. Large crown 8vo, 12s. 6d cloth.

" The most comprehensive compendium of wood working machinery we have seen. The author is a thorough master of his subject "—*Building News*

Saw Mills.

SAW MILLS. Their Arrangement and Management, and the Economical Conversion of Timber. (Being a Companion Volume to the above) By M Powis Bale, A.M. Inst C.E., M.I.M.E With numerous Illustrations Crown 8vo, 10s. 6d. cloth.

" We could not desire a more complete or practical treatise "—*Builder*

Carpentering.

THE CARPENTER'S NEW GUIDE. Comprising all the Elementary Principles essential for acquiring a knowledge of Carpentry. Founded on the late PETER NICHOLSON's Standard Work A New Edition, revised by ARTHUR ASHPITEL, F S A Together with Practical Rules on Drawing, by GEORGE PYNE. With 74 Plates, 4to, £1 1s cloth.

Timber Merchant's Companion.

THE TIMBER MERCHANT'S AND BUILDER'S COM-PANION. Containing New and Copious Tables of the Reduced Weight and Measurement of Deals and Battens, of all sizes, from One to a Thousand Pieces, and the relative Price that each size bears per Lineal Foot to any given Price per Petersburg Standard Hundred, the Price per Cube Foot of Square Timber to any given Price per Load of 50 Feet, &c , &c Also a variety of other valuable information By WILLIAM DOWSING, Timber Merchant. Third Edition, Revised and Corrected Crown 8vo, 3s cloth.

"We are glad to see a third edition of these admirable tables, which for correctness and simplicity of arrangement leave nothing to be desired."—*Timber Trades Journal.*

Practical Timber Merchant.

THE PRACTICAL TIMBER MERCHANT Being a Guide for the use of Building Contractors, Surveyors, Builders, &c , comprising useful Tables for all purposes connected with the Timber Trade, Marks of Wood, Essay on the Strength of Timber, Remarks on the Growth of Timber, &c. By W RICHARDSON Fcap. 8vo, 3s 6d. cloth

To timber merchants or users this compact treatise will be found very useful "—*Illustrated Carpenter*

Tables for Packing-Case Makers.

PACKING-CASE TABLES, showing the number of Superficial Feet 10 Boxes or Packing Cases, from six inches square and upwards. By W. RICHARDSON, Timber Broker Second Edition. Oblong 4to, 3s 6d. cloth.

"Will save much labour and calculation to makers and users of packing cases "—*Grocer.*
"Invaluable labour-saving tables "—*Ironmonger*

Superficial Measurement.

THE TRADESMAN'S GUIDE TO SUPERFICIAL MEA-SUREMENT. Tables calculated from 1 to 200 inches in length, by 1 to 108 inches in breadth. For the use of Architects, Surveyors, Engineers, Timber Merchants, Builders, &c. By JAMES HAWKINGS. Third Edition. Fcap , 3s. 6d. cloth.

MINING AND MINING INDUSTRIES.

Mining in the United Kingdom.

BRITISH MINING : A Treatise on the History, Discovery, Practical Development, and Future Prospects of Metalliferous Mines in the United Kingdom. By ROBERT HUNT, F.R S , Keeper of Mining Records : Editor of "Ure's Dictionary of Arts, Manufactures, and Mines," &c. Upwards of 950 pp , with 230 Illustrations Super-royal 8vo, £3 3s. cloth

"One of the most valuable works of reference of modern times Mr Hunt, as keeper of mining records of the United Kingdom, has had opportunities for such a task not enjoyed by anyone else, and has evidently made the most of them . The language and style adopted are good, and the treatment of the various subjects laborious, conscientious, and scientific."—*Engineering*

" A mass of information not elsewhere available, and of the greatest value to those who may be interested in our great mineral industries "—*Engineer*

Coal and Iron.

THE COAL AND IRON INDUSTRIES OF THE UNITED
KINGDOM   Comprising a Description of the Coal Fields, with Returns
of their Produce and its Distribution, and Analyses of Special Varieties
Also an Account of the occurrence of Iron Ores in Veins or Seams,
Analyses of each Variety ; and a History of the Rise and Progress of Pig
Iron Manufacture since the year 1740   By RICHARD MEADE, Assistant
Keeper of Mining Records   With Maps of the Coal Fields and Ironstone
Deposits of the United Kingdom.   8vo, £1 8s cloth.

"The book is one which must find a place on the shelves of all interested in coal and iron
production, and in the iron, steel, and other metallurgical industries "—*Engineer*

Metalliferous Minerals and Mining.

TREATISE ON METALLIFEROUS MINERALS AND
MINING   By D. C. DAVIES, F G S, Mining Engineer, &c   Author of
"A Treatise on Slate and Slate Quarrying."   Illustrated with numerous
Wood Engravings.   Third Edition, carefully Revised.   Crown 8vo,
12s 6d cloth

'As a history of the present state of mining throughout the world this book has a real
value, and it supplies an actual want, for no such information has hitherto been brought
together within such limited space '— *Athenæum*

Earthy Minerals and Mining.

A TREATISE ON EARTHY AND OTHER MINERALS
AND MINING   By D C DAVIES, F G S   Uniform with, and forming a
Companion Volume to the same Author's "Metalliferous Minerals and
Mining "   With 76 Wood Engravings.   Crown 8vo, 12s 6d cloth

"It is essentially a practical work, intended primarily for the use of practical men
We do not remember to have met with any English work on mining matters that contains the
same amount of information packed in equally convenient form "—*Academy*

Prospecting.

THE PROSPECTOR'S HANDBOOK   A Guide for the
Prospector and Traveller in Search of Metal-bearing or other Valuable
Minerals   By J W ANDERSON, M A (Camb.), F R G.S.   Second Edi-
tion, Revised   Small crown 8vo, 3s. 6d cloth.   [*Just published*

' This little work will be found, we think, to supply a much felt want, especially among
Colonists , it will also afford aid to many others who possess a taste for geological research
The book is the best of its kind —*Engineer*

Underground Pumping Machinery.

MINE DRAINAGE   Being   a   Complete   and   Practical
Treatise on Direct-Acting Underground Steam Pumping Machinery,
with a Description of a large number of the best known Engines, their
General Utility and the Special Sphere of their Action, &c., &c   By
STEPHEN MICHELL   8vo, 15s cloth

"It is a most valuable work, and stands almost alone in the literature of steam pumping
machinery "—*Colliery Guardian*

Coal Mining.

COAL AND COAL MINING · A Rudimentary Treatise on.
By WARINGTON W SMYTH, M A, F.R S, &c., Chief Inspector of the
Mines of the Crown.   Sixth Edition, Revised and Enlarged.   With
numerous Illustrations.   12mo, 4s cloth boards   [*Just published*

As an outline is given of every known coal field in this and other countries, as well as of
the principal methods of working, the book will doubtless interest a very large number of
readers "—*Mining Journal*

NAVAL ARCHITECTURE, NAVIGATION, etc.

Pocket-Book for Naval Architects & Shipbuilders.

THE NAVAL ARCHITECT'S AND SHIPBUILDER'S POCKET-BOOK of Formulæ, Rules, and Tables, and Marine Engineer's and Surveyor's Handy Book of Reference By CLEMENT MACKROW, Member of the Institution of Naval Architects, Naval Draughtsman Third Edition, Revised With numerous Diagrams, &c. Fcap , 12s 6d strongly bound in leather.

Should be used by all who are engaged in the construction or design of vessels . . Will be found to contain the most useful tables and formulæ required by shipbuilders carefully collected from the best authorities, and put together in a popular and simple form — *Engineer*

' The professional shipbuilder has now, in a convenient and accessible form, reliable data or solving many of the numerous problems that present themselves in the course of his work ' —*Iron*

' There is scarcely a subject on which a naval architect or shipbuilder can require to refresh his memory which will not be found within the covers of Mr Mackrow's book —*English Mechanic*

Pocket-Book for Marine Engineers.

A POCKET-BOOK OF USEFUL TABLES AND FORMULÆ FOR MARINE ENGINEERS By FRANK PROCTOR, A I N.A. Third Edition. Royal 32mo, leather, gilt edges, with strap, 4s

' A most useful companion to all marine engineers —*United Service Gazette.*

Marine Engines, &c.

MARINE ENGINES AND STEAM VESSELS A Treatise on By ROBERT MURRAY, C E , Principal Officer to the Board of Trade for the East Coast of Scotland District. Eighth Edition, thoroughly Revised, with considerable Additions, by the Author and by GEORGE CARLISLE, C E , Senior Surveyor to the Board of Trade at Liverpool. 12mo, 5s. cloth boards

' As a compendious and useful guide to engineers of our mercantile and royal naval services, we should say it cannot be surpassed —*Building News*

Lighthouses.

EUROPEAN LIGHTHOUSE SYSTEMS Being a Report of a Tour of Inspection made in 1873 By Major GEORGE H ELLIOT, Corps of Engineers, U S.A. Illustrated by 51 Engravings and 31 Woodcuts 8vo, 21s cloth

Navigation (Practical), with Tables.

PRACTICAL NAVIGATION Consisting of the Sailor's Sea-Book, by JAMES GREENWOOD and W H ROSSER; together with the requisite Mathematical and Nautical Tables for the Working of the Problems, by HENRY LAW, C E., and Professor J R. YOUNG. Illustrated. 12mo, 7s strongly half-bound

---

The following books on NAVAL ARCHITECTURE, etc. are published in WEALE'S RUDIMENTARY SERIES.

MASTING, MAST-MAKING, AND RIGGING OF SHIPS By ROBERT KIPPING, N A. Fifteenth Edition 12mo, 2s. 6d. cloth boards.

SAILS AND SAIL MAKING. Eleventh Edition, Enlarged, with an Appendix. By ROBERT KIPPING, N A. Illustrated. 12mo, 3s. cloth boards

NAVAL ARCHITECTURE By JAMES PEAKE. Fifth Edition, with Plates and Diagrams. 12mo, 4s. cloth boards.

NATURAL PHILOSOPHY AND SCIENCE.

Dr. LARDNER'S HANDBOOKS OF NATURAL PHILOSOPHY.

*** *The following five volumes, though each is complete in itself, and to be purchased separately, form* A COMPLETE COURSE OF NATURAL PHILOSOPHY. *The style is studiously popular.   It has been the author's aim to supply Manuals for the Student, the Engineer, the Artisan, and the superior classes in Schools.*

THE HANDBOOK OF MECHANICS.   By DIONYSIUS LARD-
NER, D C L , formerly Professor of Natural Philosophy and Astronomy in University College, London   Enlarged and almost Rewritten by BENJAMIN LOEWY, F.R.A.S.   With 378 Illustrations   Post 8vo, 6s cloth
" Mr Loewy has carefully revised the book, and brought it up to modern requirements "
—*Nature*

The HANDBOOK of HYDROSTATICS AND PNEUMATICS.
By Dr. LARDNER   New Edition, Revised and Enlarged, by BENJAMIN LOEWY, F R A S   With 236 Illustrations.   Post 8vo, 5s cloth.
" For those who desire to obtain an accurate knowledge of physical science without the profound methods of mathematical investigation, this work is not merely intended, but well adapted '—*Chemical News*

THE HANDBOOK OF HEAT   By Dr LARDNER.   Edited
and almost entirely Rewritten by BENJAMIN LOEWY, F.R.A.S., &c.   117 Illustrations   Post 8vo, 6s cloth.
" The style is always clear and precise, and conveys instruction without leaving any cloudiness or lurking doubts behind '—*Engineering*

THE HANDBOOK OF OPTICS   By Dr. LARDNER.   New
Edition.   Edited by T OLVER HARDING, B A , of University College, London.   With 298 Illustrations.   Small 8vo, 448 pages, 5s cloth.
" Written by one of the ablest English scientific writers, beautifully and elaborately illus-trated '—*Mechanics' Magazine*

THE HANDBOOK OF ELECTRICITY, MAGNETISM, AND ACOUSTICS. By Dr. LARDNER. Ninth Thousand.   Edited by GEORGE CAREY FOSTER, B.A , F.C.S. With 400 Illustrations.   Small 8vo, 5s cloth
" The book could not have been entrusted to anyone better calculated to preserve the terse and lucid style of Lardner, while correcting his errors and bringing up his work to the present state of scientific knowledge '—*Popular Science Review*

Dr. Lardner's Handbook of Astronomy.

THE HANDBOOK OF ASTRONOMY   By DIONYSIUS
LARDNER, D C L , formerly Professor of Natural Philosophy and As-tronomy in University College, London.   Fourth Edition, Revised and Edited by EDWIN DUNKIN, F R.A S., Royal Observatory, Greenwich With 38 Plates and upwards of 100 Woodcuts.   In One Vol , small 8vo, 550 pages, 9s. 6d. cloth
" Probably no other book contains the same amount of information in so compendious and well arranged a form—certainly none at the price at which this is offered to the public "—
Athenæum

The Blowpipe.

THE BLOWPIPE in CHEMISTRY, MINERALOGY, AND GEOLOGY.   Containing all known Methods of Anhydrous Analysis, many working Examples, and Instructions for Making Apparatus.   By Lieutenant Colonel W. A. Ross, R.A , F.G.S.   With 120 Illustrations. Crown 8vo, 3s 6d cloth
" The student who goes conscientiously through the course of experimentation here laid down will gain a better insight into inorganic chemistry and mineralogy than if he had 'got up' any of the best text books of the day, and passed any number of examinations in their contents "—*Chemical News.*

Electricity.

A MANUAL OF ELECTRICITY : Including Galvanism,
Magnetism, Dia-Magnetism, Electro-Dynamics, Magno-Electricity, and the
Electric Telegraph By HENRY M. NOAD, Ph D , F R.S., F.C.S Fourth
Edition. With 500 Woodcuts 8vo, £1 4s cloth.

"The accounts given of electricity and galvanism are not only complete in a scientific
sense, but, which is a rarer thing, are popular and interesting "—*Lancet*

Text-Book of Electricity.

THE STUDENT'S TEXT-BOOK OF ELECTRICITY By
HENRY M NOAD, Ph D , F R S , F C S New Edition, carefully Revised
With an Introduction and Additional Chapters, by W H PREECE,
M.I C E , Vice-President of the Society of Telegraph Engineers, &c.
With 470 Illustrations Crown 8vo, 12s 6d cloth

"We can recommend Dr Noad's book for clear style, great range of subject a good
index, and a plethora of woodcuts Such a collection is indispensable —*Athenæum*
"An admirable text-book for every student—beginner or advanced—of electricity —
Engineering

MATHEMATICS, GEOMETRY, TABLES, etc.

Practical Mathematics.

MATHEMATICS FOR PRACTICAL MEN. Being a Com-
mon-place Book of Pure and Mixed Mathematics. Designed chiefly for
the Use of Civil Engineers, Architects, and Surveyors With an Appendix of copious Logarithmic and other Tables By OLINTHUS GREG-
ORY, LL D , F R A S , Enlarged by HENRY LAW, C.E 4th Edition,
carefully Revised by J. R YOUNG, formerly Professor of Mathematics,
Belfast College With 13 Plates, 8vo, £1 1s cloth.

"The engineer or architect will here find ready to his hand rules for solving nearly every
mathematical difficulty that may arise in his practice The rules are in all cases explained by
means of examples in which every step in the process is clearly worked out '—*Builder*.

Metrical Units and Systems, etc.

MODERN METROLOGY : A Manual of the Metrical Units
and Systems of the Present Century With an Appendix containing a proposed English System By LEWIS D'A. JACKSON, A M. Inst C E , Author
of "Aid to Survey Practice," &c. Large crown 8vo, 12s. 6d. cloth.

"For exhaustive tables of equivalent weights and measures of all sorts, and for clear de-
monstrations of the effects of the various systems that have been proposed or adopted, Mr
Jackson's treatise is without a rival "—*Academy*

The Metric System.

A SERIES OF METRIC TABLES, in which the British
Standard Measures and Weights are compared with those of the Metric
System at present in Use on the Continent By C. H DOWLING, C.E
Second Edition, Revised and Enlarged 8vo, 10s. 6d. strongly bound

"Their accuracy has been certified by Professor Airy, the Astronomer Royal "—*Builder*

Geometry for the Architect, Engineer, etc.

PRACTICAL GEOMETRY, for the Architect, Engineer and
Mechanic. Giving Rules for the Delineation and Application of various
Geometrical Lines, Figures and Curves. By E. W TARN, M A , Archi-
tect. Second Edition. With Appendices on Diagrams of Strains and
Isometrical Projection. With 172 Illustrations, demy 8vo, 9s cloth

"This is a manual for the practical man, whether architect, engineer, or mechanic.
The object of the author being to avoid all abstruse formulæ or complicated methods, and to
enable persons with but a moderate knowledge of geometry to work out the problems required "—*English Mechanic*

Number and Weight Calculator.

THE COMBINED NUMBER AND WEIGHT CALCU-LATOR Containing upwards of Two Hundred and Fifty Thousand separate Calculations showing at a glance the value at 421 different rates, ranging from $\frac{1}{32}$ of a penny to 20s each, or per cwt., and £20 per ton, of any Number of Articles consecutively, from 1-470 Any number of cwts , qrs , and lbs , from 1 cwt. to 470 cwts Any number of tons, cwts , qrs , and lbs , from 1 to 23½ tons. For the use of Accountants and Auditors, Railway Companies, Canal Companies, Shippers, Shipping Agents, General Carriers, &c , Ironfounders, Brass founders, Metal Merchants, Iron Manufacturers, Ironmongers, Engineers, Machinists, Boiler Makers, Millwrights, Roofing, Bridge and Girder Makers, Colliery Proprietors, &c , Timber Merchants, Builders, Contractors, Architects, Surveyors, Auctioneers, Valuers, Brokers, Mill Owners and Manufacturers, Mill Furnishers, Merchants, and general Wholesale Tradesmen.   By WILLIAM CHADWICK, Public Accountant   Imp. 8vo, 30s strongly half-bound.   [*Just published*

Comprehensive Weight Calculator.

THE WEIGHT CALCULATOR. Being a Series of Tables upon a New and Comprehensive Plan, exhibiting at One Reference the exact Value of any Weight from 1 lb. to 15 tons, at 300 Progressive Rates, from 1d to 168s per cwt , and containing 186,000 Direct Answers, which, with their Combinations, consisting of a single addition (mostly to be performed at sight), will afford an aggregate of 10,266,000 Answers , the whole being calculated and designed to ensure correctness and promote despatch   By HENRY HARBEN, Accountant, Sheffield, Author of "The Discount Guide "   An entirely New Edition, carefully Revised. Royal 8vo, strongly half bound, £1 5s

" A practical and useful work of reference for men of business generally ; it is the best of the kind we have seen   We have frequently been asked if such a work as this could be obtained, and therefore refer to it with pleasure ' —*Ironmonger*

Comprehensive Discount Guide.

THE DISCOUNT GUIDE. Comprising several Series of Tables for the use of Merchants, Manufacturers, Ironmongers, and others, by which may be ascertained the exact Profit arising from any mode of using Discounts, either in the Purchase or Sale of Goods, and the method of either Altering a Rate of Discount or Advancing a Price, so as to produce, by one operation, a sum that will realise any required profit after allowing one or more Discounts , to which are added Tables of Profit or Advance from 1¼ to 90 per cent , Tables of Discount from 1¼ to 98¾ per cent , and Tables of Commission, &c , from ⅛ to 10 per cent. By HENRY HARBEN, Accountant, Author of "The Weight Calculator " New Edition, carefully Revised and Corrected. Demy 8vo, 544 pp , half-bound, £1 5s.

" All these tables are well arranged and clearly printed , and the collection will be found of great value in those businesses for which the book has been especially compiled "—*Engineering*

Iron and Metal Trades' Calculator.

THE IRON AND METAL TRADES' COMPANION Being a Calculator, containing a Series of Tables upon a New and Comprehensive Plan, for expeditiously ascertaining the Value of any Goods bought or sold by Weight, from 1s per cwt to 112s. per cwt , and from one farthing per pound to one shilling per pound   Each Table extends from one pound to 100 tons   To which are appended Rules on Decimals, Square and Cube Root, Mensuration of Superficies and Solids, &c. , also Tables of Weights of Materials, and other Useful Memoranda. By THOMAS DOWNIE. Strongly bound in leather, 396 pp , 9s

" A most useful set of tables, and will supply a want, for nothing like them before existed '—*Building News*

Iron Shipbuilders' and Iron Merchants' Tables.

IRON-PLATE WEIGHT TABLES For Iron Shipbuilders, Engineers and Iron Merchants. Containing the Calculated Weights of upwards of 150,000 different sizes of Iron Plates, from 1 foot by 6 in by ¼ in to 10 feet by 5 feet by 1 in Worked out on the basis of 40 lbs to the square foot of Iron of 1 inch in thickness. Carefully Compiled and thoroughly Revised by H. BURLINSON and W. H SIMPSON Oblong 4to 25s. half-bound.

"This work will be found of great utility The authors have had much practical experi ence of what is wanting in making estimates, and the use of the book will save much time in making elaborate calculations "—*English Mechanic*

INDUSTRIAL AND USEFUL ARTS.

Electro-Deposition.

ELECTRO-DEPOSITION A Practical Treatise on the Electrolysis of Gold, Silver. Copper, Nickel, and other Metals, and Alloys With descriptions of Voltaic Batteries, Magneto- and Dynamo-Electric Machines, Thermopiles, and of the Materials and Processes used in every department of the Art, and several chapters on Electro-Metallurgy By ALEXANDER WATT, Author of "Electro-Metallurgy," 'The Art of Soap-making," &c, &c With numerous Illustrations. Crown 8vo, nearly 600 pp, 12s 6d. cloth. [*Just published.*

Soap-making.

THE ART OF SOAP-MAKING A Practical Handbook of the Manufacture of Hard and Soft Soaps, Toilet Soaps, &c Including many New Processes, and a Chapter on the Recovery of Glycerine from Waste Leys By ALEXANDER WATT, Author of "Electro-Metallurgy Practically Treated," &c. With numerous Illustrations Second Edition, carefully Revised Crown 8vo, 9s cloth. [*Just published.*

"The work will prove very useful, not merely to the technological student, but to the practical soapboiler who wishes to understand the theory of his art "—*Chemical News*

' Mr Watt's book is a thoroughly practical treatise on an art which has almost no literature in our language We congratulate the author on the success of his endeavour to fill a void in English technical literature '—*Nature*

Leather Manufacture.

THE ART OF LEATHER MANUFACTURE Being a Practical Handbook, in which the Operations of Tanning, Currying, and Leather Dressing are fully Described, and the Principles of Tanning Explained, and many Recent Processes introduced; as also Methods for the Estimation of Tannin, and a Description of the Arts of Glue Boiling, Gut Dressing, &c By ALEXANDER WATT, Author of "Soap-Making," "Electro-Metallurgy," &c. With numerous Illustrations. Crown 8vo, 12s 6d cloth [*Just published.*

"Every item of use and interest to the leather trade has been touched upon, and the descriptions and explanations of the various processes are exhaustively given '—*Tanners and Curriers' Journal*

Boot and Shoe Making.

THE ART OF BOOT AND SHOE-MAKING. A Practical Handbook, including Measurement, Last-Fitting, Cutting-Out, Closing and Making, with a Description of the most approved Machinery employed By JOHN B LENO, late Editor of *St Crispin*, and *The Boot and Shoe-Maker* With numerous Illustrations. Crown 8vo, 5s cloth.
[*Just published.*

"A very complete account of the art and science of bootmaking which includes all that need be said about leathers and other materials as well as about hand tools and the various machines that have latterly been introduced to supplement or supersede the old fashioned handiwork."—*Weekly Dispatch*

C

Dentistry.

MECHANICAL DENTISTRY   A Practical Treatise on the Construction of the various kinds of Artificial Dentures. Comprising also Useful Formulæ, Tables and Receipts for Gold Plate Clasps, Solders, &c., &c. By CHARLES HUNTER. Second Edition, Revised. With upwards of 100 Wood Engravings. Crown 8vo, 7s. 6d. cloth

"An authoritative treatise   We can strongly recommend Mr. Hunter's treatise to all students preparing for the profession of dentistry, as well as to every mechanical dentist."— *Dublin Journal of Dental Science*
' A work in a concise form that few could read without gaining information from —*British Journal of Dental Science*

Brewing.

A HANDBOOK FOR YOUNG BREWERS. By HERBERT EDWARDS WRIGHT, B.A. Crown 8vo, 3s. 6d. cloth.

" This little volume, containing such a large amount of good sense in so small a compass, ought to recommend itself to every brewery pupil, and many who have passed that stage — *Brewers' Guardian*

Electroplating, etc.

ELECTROPLATING · A Practical Handbook. By J. W. URQUHART, C E   With numerous Illustrations   Crown 8vo, 5s cloth.

" The information given appears to be based on direct personal knowledge .   Its science is sound and the style is always clear "—*Athenæum*

Electrotyping, etc.

ELECTROTYPING   The Reproduction and Multiplication o Printing Surfaces and Works of Art by the Electro-deposition of Metals. By J W URQUHART, C E   Crown 8vo, 5s cloth

" In this work the author enters systematically and thoroughly into every department of the process, in the style of one who combines theory with practice   We can recommend this treatise, not merely to amateurs, but to those actually engaged in the trade '—*Chemical News.*

Electric Lighting.

ELECTRIC LIGHT   Its Production and Use. Embodying Plain Directions for the Treatment of Voltaic Batteries, Electric Lamps, and Dynamo-Electric Machines   By J. W URQUHART, C E , Author of "Electroplating   A Practical Handbook "   Edited by F C WEBB. M I C E , M S.T E   Second Edition, Revised, with large Additions and 128 Illustrations   7s 6d cloth
' The book is by far the best that we have yet met with on the subject '—*Athenæum*

Goldsmiths' Work.

THE   GOLDSMITH'S   HANDBOOK   Containing full Instructions in the Art of Alloying, Melting, Reducing, Colouring, Collecting and Refining   The processes of Manipulation, Recovery of Waste, Chemical and Physical Properties of Gold, with a New System of Mixing its Alloys, Solders, Enamels, and other useful Rules and Recipes, &c   By GEORGE E GEE   Third Edition, considerably enlarged.   12mo, 3s 6d cloth boards.

" The best work yet printed on its subject for a reasonable price   We have no doubt that it will speedily become a standard book which few will care to be without —*Jeweller and Metal-worker*

Silversmiths' Work.

THE SILVERSMITH'S HANDBOOK   Containing full Instructions for the Alloying and Working of Silver, including the different modes of Refining and Melting the Metal, its Solders, the Preparation of Imitation Alloys, Methods of Manipulation, &c., &c.   By GEORGE E. GEE, Jeweller, &c. Second Edition, Revised, with numerous Illustrations   12mo, 3s. 6d cloth boards

" The chief merit of the work is its practical character . .   The workers in the trade will speedily discover its merits when they sit down to study it —*English Mechanic*

** *The two preceding Works, in One handsome Vol., half-bound, entitled* "THE GOLDSMITH'S AND SILVERSMITH'S COMPLETE HANDBOOK," 7s.

[*Just published*

CHEMICAL MANUFACTURES AND COMMERCE.

Alkali Trade, Manufacture of Sulphuric Acid, etc.

A MANUAL OF THE ALKALI TRADE, including the Manufacture of Sulphuric Acid, Sulphate of Soda, and Bleaching Powder. By JOHN LOMAS, Alkali Manufacturer, Newcastle-upon-Tyne and London. With 232 Illustrations and Working Drawings, and containing nearly 400 pages of Text. Second Edition, with Additions. Super-royal 8vo, 30s cloth.

' The author has given the fullest, most practical, and, to all concerned in the alkali trade most valuable mass of information that, to our knowledge, has been published in any language —*Engineer*

' The book is written by a manufacturer for manufacturers Every step in the manufacture is very fully described in this manual, and each improvement explained Everything which tends to introduce economy into the technical details of this trade receives the fullest attention '—*Athenæum.*

Alkali Tables.

ALKALI TABLES A Ready Reckoner for the use of Chemical Merchants, Manufacturers and Brokers By OSWIN BELL Second Edition. 32mo, 1s Paper wrapper. [*Just published*

Commercial Chemical Analysis.

THE COMMERCIAL HANDBOOK OF CHEMICAL AN-ALYSIS or, Practical Instructions for the determination of the Intrinsic or Commercial Value of Substances used in Manufactures, in Trades and in the Arts By A NORMANDY New Edition, Enlarged and to a great extent Re-written, by HENRY M. NOAD, Ph.D, F R S. With numerous Illustrations Crown 8vo, 12s 6d cloth

"Essential to the analysts appointed under the new Act The most recent results are given, and the work is well edited and carefully written "—*Nature*

Dye-Wares and Colours.

THE MANUAL OF COLOURS AND DYE-WARES : *Their Properties, Applications, Valuation, Impurities, and Sophistications.* For the use of Dyers, Printers, Drysalters, Brokers, &c. By J W. SLATER Second Edition, Revised and greatly Enlarged. Crown 8vo, 7s 6d cloth.

"Practical dyers, &c , will welcome the work in its improved form There is no other work in the language which covers precisely the same ground To technological students preparing for examinations in dyeing and printing it will prove exceedingly useful, '—*Chemical News.*

AUCTIONEERING, ESTATE AGENCY, etc.

Auctioneer's Assistant.

THE APPRAISER, AUCTIONEER, BROKER, HOUSE AND ESTATE AGENT AND VALUER'S POCKET ASSISTANT, for the Valuation for Purchase, Sale, or Renewal of Leases, Annuities and Reversions, and of property generally, with Prices for Inventories, &c By JOHN WHEELER, Valuer, &c Fifth Edition, Re-written and greatly Extended by C. NORRIS, Surveyor, Valuer, &c Royal 32mo, 5s cloth.

"Cram full of valuable information of practical value It is a trustworthy and compendious guide to all sorts of valuation "—*Insurance Agent*

Auctioneering.

AUCTIONEERS : Their Duties and Liabilities   By ROBERT SQUIBBS, Auctioneer. Demy 8vo, 10s. 6d. cloth.

" The position and duties of auctioneers are treated compendiously and clearly '—*Builder*

" Every auctioneer ought to possess a copy of this excellent work. '—*Ironmonger*

House Property.

HANDBOOK OF HOUSE PROPERTY   A Popular and Practical Guide to the Purchase, Mortgage, Tenancy and Compulsory Sale of Houses and Land   By E. L. TARBUCK, Architect and Surveyor Fourth Edition, Revised and Enlarged.   [*In preparation.*

" The advice is thoroughly practical '—*Law Journal*

" This is a well-written and thoughtful work   We commend the work to the careful study of all interested in questions affecting houses and land '—*Land Agents' Record*

Inwood's Estate Tables.

TABLES FOR THE PURCHASING OF ESTATES, Freehold, Copyhold, or Leasehold ; Annuities, Advowsons, &c ; together with SMART'S Five Tables of Compound Interest, and an Extension of the same to Lower and Intermediate Rates   By W. INWOOD. 22nd Edition, with considerable Additions, and new and valuable Tables of Logarithms for the more Difficult Computations of the Interest of Money, Discount, Annuities, &c , by M. FEDOR THOMAN, of the Société Crédit Mobilier of Paris. 12mo, 8s. cloth.

" Those interested in the purchase and sale of estates, and in the adjustment of compensation cases, as well as in transactions in annuities, life insurance, &c , will find the present edition of eminent service "—*Engineering*

A Complete Epitome of the Laws of this Country.

EVERY MAN'S OWN LAWYER   A Handy-book of the Principles of Law and Equity. By A BARRISTER. Twenty-fourth Edition, carefully revised and brought down to the end of the last Session (1886), including Summaries of the latest Statute Laws   With Notes and References to the Authorities   Crown 8vo, price 6s. 8d (saved at every consultation), strongly bound in cloth

Comprising THE RIGHTS AND WRONGS OF INDIVIDUALS—MERCANTILE AND COMMERCIAL LAW—CRIMINAL LAW—PARISH LAW—COUNTY COURT LAW—GAME AND FISHERY LAWS—POOR MEN'S LAWSUITS—THE LAWS OF BANKRUPTCY—BETS AND WAGERS—CHEQUES, BILLS, AND NOTES—CONTRACTS AND AGREEMENTS—COPYRIGHT—ELECTIONS AND REGISTRATIONS—INSURANCE—LIBEL AND SLANDER—MARRIAGE AND DIVORCE—MERCHANT SHIPPING—MORTGAGES—SETTLEMENTS—STOCK EXCHANGE PRACTICE—TRADE MARKS AND PATENTS—TRESPASS—NUISANCES, &c —TRANSFER OF LAND, &c —WARRANTY—WILLS AND AGREEMENTS, &c &c

Also, Law for Landlord and Tenant—Master and Servant—Workmen and Apprentices—Heirs—Devisees and Legatees—Husband and Wife—Executors and Trustees—Guardian and Ward—Married Women and Infants—Partners and Agents—Lender, Borrower and Sureties—Debtor and Creditor—Purchaser and Vendor—Companies and Associations—Friendly Societies—Clergymen—Churchwardens—Medical Practitioners, &c —Bankers—Farmers—Contractors—Stock and Share Brokers—Sportsmen—Gamekeepers—Farriers and Horse Dealers—Auctioneers—House Agents—Innkeepers, &c —Bakers—Millers &c —Pawnbrokers—Surveyors—Railways and Carriers—Constables—Seamen—Soldiers, &c &c

Opinions of the Press.

" *No Englishman ought to be without this book*   Any person perfectly uninformed on legal matters, who may require sound information on unknown law points, will, by reference to this book, acquire the necessary information, and thus on many occasions save the expense and loss of time of a visit to a lawyer "—*Engineer*

" It s a complete code of English Law, written in plain language which all can understand   Should be in the hands of every business man, and all who wish to abolish lawyers' bills '—*Weekly Times*

" A useful and concise epitome of the law, compiled with considerable care '—*Law Magazine*

" What it professes to be—a complete epitome of the laws of this country, thoroughly intelligible to non-professional readers   The book is a handy one to have in read mess when some knotty point requires ready so ution."—*Pell s Life*

A NEW LIST OF

WEALE'S

RUDIMENTARY SCIENTIFIC SERIES

Comprising Works in almost every department of

INDUSTRY, SCIENCE AND ART,

PUBLISHED BY

CROSBY LOCKWOOD & CO.,

7, Stationers' Hall Court, E.C.

The books are bound in limp cloth throughout, unless otherwise stated, but those marked with a ‡ may be had strongly bound in cloth boards for 6d. extra.
*₊⁻ In ordering please quote the numbers as well as the titles and prices.

CIVIL ENGINEERING, SURVEYING, etc.

31. *Wells and Well-Sinking.* By JOHN GEORGE SWINDELL, A.R.I.B.A., and G. R. BURNELL, C.E. Revised Edition. With a New Appendix on the Qualities of Water. Illustrated. 2s.

35. *The Blasting and Quarrying of Stone,* for Building and other Purposes. With Remarks on the Blowing up of Bridges. By Gen. Sir JOHN BURGOYNE, Bart., K C.B. Illustrated. 1s. 6d.

43. *Tubular, and other Iron Girder Bridges,* particularly describing the Britannia and Conway Tubular Bridges. By G. DRYSDALE DEMPSEY, C.E. Fourth Edition. 2s.

44. *Foundations and Concrete Works,* with Practical Remarks on Footings, Sand, Concrete, Béton, Pile-driving, Caissons, and Cofferdams, &c. By E. DOBSON. Fifth Edition. 1s. 6d.

60. *Land and Engineering Surveying.* By T. BAKER, C.E. New Edition, revised by EDWARD NUGENT, C.E. 2s.‡

80*.*Embanking Lands from the Sea.* With Examples and Particulars of actual Embankments, &c. By J. WIGGINS, F.G.S. 2s.

81. *Water Works,* for the Supply of Cities and Towns. With a Description of the Principal Geological Formations of England as influencing Supplies of Water; and Details of Engines and Pumping Machinery for raising Water. By SAMUEL HUGHES, F.G.S., C.E. New Edition. 4s.‡

MECHANICAL ENGINEERING, etc.

MECHANICAL ENGINEERING, ETC , *continued*

165. *Iron and Heat,* exhibiting the Principles concerned in the Construction of Iron Beams, Pillars, and Bridge Girders, and the Action of Heat in the Smelting Furnace. By J. ARMOUR, C E　2s. 6d ‡

166. *Power in Motion :* Horse-Power, Toothed-Wheel Gearing, Long and Short Driving Bands, and Angular Forces. By J ARMOUR. 2s. 6d ‡

171. *The Workman's Manual of Engineering Drawing.* By J MAXTON. 6th Edition　With 7 Plates and 350 Cuts　3s 6d ‡

190. *Steam and the Steam Engine,* Stationary and Portable. By JOHN SEWELL and D K. CLARK, M.I C.E　3s. 6d.‡

200. *Fuel :* Its Combustion and Economy　By C W. WILLIAMS　With Recent Practice in the Combustion and Economy of Fuel—Coal, Coke, Wood, Peat, Petroleum, &c　By D K CLARK, M I C E　Third Edition, Revised. 3s 6d ‡　　[*Just published.*

202 *Locomotive Engines.* By G. D. DEMPSEY, C.E. With large Additions by D. KINNEAR CLARK, M I.C.E. 3s ‡

211. *The Boilermaker's Assistant* in Drawing, Templating, and Calculating Boiler and Tank Work　By JOHN COURTNEY, Practical Boiler Maker. Edited by D. K. CLARK, C E　100 Illustrations　2s.

217. *Sewing Machinery :* Its Construction, History, &c , with Full Technical Directions for Adjusting, &c. By J. W URQUHART, C E. 2s ‡

223. *Mechanical Engineering.* Comprising Metallurgy, Moulding, Casting, Forging, Tools, Workshop Machinery, Manufacture of the Steam Engine, &c. By FRANCIS CAMPIN, C E 2s 6d.‡

236. *Details of Machinery.* Comprising Instructions for the Execution of various Works in Iron. By FRANCIS CAMPIN, C E. 3s ‡

237 *The Smithy and Forge ;* Including the Farrier's Art and Coach Smithing. By W J E CRANE Illustrated. 2s 6d ‡

238 *The Sheet-Metal Worker's Guide :* A Practical Handbook for Tinsmiths, Coppersmiths, Zincworkers, &c　With 94 Diagrams and Working Patterns　By W. J. E CRANE. 1s. 6d.

251. *Steam and Machinery Management :* With Hints on Construction and Selection　By M POWIS BALE, M I M E 2s 6d ‡

254. *The Boilermaker's Ready-Reckoner.* With Examples of Practical Geometry and Templating By JOHN COURTNEY. Edited by D. K CLARK, M.Inst.C.E. 4s. limp, 5s. half-bound

255. *Locomotive Engine-Driving.* A Practical Manual for Engineers in charge of Locomotive Engines　By MICHAEL REYNOLDS, M S E　Seventh Edition　3s 6d. limp, 4s 6d cloth boards　　[*Just published.*

256. *Stationary Engine-Driving.* A Practical Manual for Engineers in charge of Stationary Engines　By MICHAEL REYNOLDS, M.S.E.　Third Edition. 3s. 6d. limp, 4s. 6d. cloth. [*Just published.*

MINING, METALLURGY, etc.

4 *Mineralogy,* Rudiments of : A Concise View of the General Properties of Minerals By A RAMSAY, F G S, F R G S, &c Third Edition, revised and enlarged Illustrated 3s 6d ‡
[Just published

117. *Subterraneous Surveying,* Elementary and Practical Treatise on, with and without the Magnetic Needle. By THOMAS FENWICK, Surveyor of Mines, and THOMAS BAKER, C E Illustrated 2s. 6d

133. *Metallurgy of Copper :* An Introduction to the Methods of Seeking, Mining, and Assaying Copper, and Manufacturing its Alloys By ROBERT H. LAMBORN, Ph D Woodcuts 2s 6d ‡

135. *Electro-Metallurgy,* Practically Treated. By ALEXANDER WATT, F R S S A Eighth Edition, revised, with additional Matter and Illustrations, including the most recent Processes 3s ‡

172. *Mining Tools,* Manual of. For the Use of Mine Managers, Agents, Students, &c By WILLIAM MORGANS. 2s. 6d ‡

172* *Mining Tools, Atlas* of Engravings to Illustrate the above, containing 235 Illustrations, drawn to Scale 4to 4s 6d., cloth boards, 6s

176. *Metallurgy of Iron.* Containing History of Iron Manufacture, Methods of Assay, and Analyses of Iron Ores, Processes of Manufacture of Iron and Steel, &c. By H BAUERMAN, F G S Fifth Edition, revised and enlarged 5s ‡

180. *Coal and Coal Mining.* By WARINGTON W. SMYTH, M A , F.R S Sixth Edition, revised 3s. 6d ‡ *[Just published*

195. *The Mineral Surveyor and Valuer's Complete Guide,* with New Traverse Tables, and Descriptions of Improved Instruments, also the Correct Principles of Laying out and Valuing Mineral Properties By WILLIAM LINTERN, Mining and Civil Engineer 3s 6d ‡

214. *Slate and Slate Quarrying,* Scientific, Practical and Commercial. By D C DAVIES, F G S , Mining Engineer, &c. 3s ‡

220. *Magnetic Surveying and Angular Surveying,* with Records of the Peculiarities of Needle Disturbances. Compiled from the Results of carefully made Experiments By W LINTERN 2s

ARCHITECTURE, BUILDING, etc.

16. *Architecture — Orders —* The Orders and their Æsthetic Principles By W H LEEDS Illustrated. 1s 6d

17. *Architecture—Styles—*The History and Description of the Styles of Architecture of Various Countries, from the Earliest to the Present Period. By T TALBOT BURY, F R.I.B.A , &c Illustrated 2s.

‚ ORDERS AND STYLES OF ARCHITECTURE, in *One Vol* , 3s 6d.

ARCHITECTURE, BUILDING, ETC , *continued*

18. *Architecture—Design*—The Principles of Design
in Architecture, as deducible from Nature and exemplified in the Works of the Greek and Gothic Architects By E. L. GARBETT, Architect Illustrated. 2s 6d

* *The three preceding Works, in One handsome Vol , half bound, entitled* "MODERN ARCHITECTURE," *price 6s.*

22. *The Art of Building,* Rudiments of. General
Principles of Construction, Materials used in Building, Strength and Use of Materials, Working Drawings, Specifications, and Estimates. By E DOBSON 2s ‡

25. *Masonry and Stonecutting* : Rudimentary Treatise
on the Principles of Masonic Projection and their application to Construction By EDWARD DOBSON, M R I B A , &c 2s 6d ‡

42. *Cottage Building.* By C. BRUCE ALLEN, Architect.
Tenth Edition, revised and enlarged, with a Chapter on Economic Cottages for Allotments by EDWARD F ALLEN, C E 2s

45. *Limes, Cements, Mortars, Concretes, Mastics,*
Plastering, &c By G. R BURNELL, C E. Twelfth Edition 1s 6d.

57. *Warming and Ventilation.* An Exposition of
the General Principles as applied to Domestic and Public Buildings, Mines, Lighthouses, Ships, &c. By C TOMLINSON, F R S , &c Illustrated. 3s

111. *Arches, Piers, Buttresses, &c. :* Experimental
Essays on the Principles of Construction. By W BLAND. Illustrated 1s 6d.

116. *The Acoustics of Public Buildings ;* or, The
Principles of the Science of Sound applied to the purposes of the Architect and Builder. By T. ROGER SMITH, M R I B A , Architect Illustrated 1s 6d.

127. *Architectural Modelling in Paper,* the Art of.
By T A. RICHARDSON, Architect. Illustrated. 1s 6d

128. *Vitruvius—the Architecture of Marcus Vitruvius*
Pollo In Ten Books Translated from the Latin by JOSEPH GWILT F S A , F.R A S With 23 Plates 5s.

130. *Grecian Architecture,* An Enquiry into the Prin-
ciples of Beauty in , with an Historical View of the Rise and Progress of the Art in Greece By the EARL OF ABERDEEN 1s

* *The two preceding Works in One handsome Vol , half-bound, entitled* "ANCIENT ARCHITECTURE," *price 6s*

132. *The Erection of Dwelling-Houses.* Illustrated by
a Perspective View, Plans, Elevations, and Sections of a pair of Semi-detached Villas, with the Specification, Quantities, and Estimates, &c By S H. BROOKS. New Edition 2s 6d ‡

156 *Quantities and Measurements,* How to Calculate
and Take them in Bricklayers', Masons', Plasterers', Plumbers', Painters', Paperhangers',Gilders', Smiths',Carpenters', and Joiners' Work By A C BEATON, Architect and Surveyor New and Enlarged Edition Illustrations 1s 6d.

ARCHITECTURE, BUILDING, ETC , *continued*

175. *Lockwood & Co.'s Builder's and Contractor's*
Price Book, containing the latest Prices of all kinds of Builders'
Materials and Labour, and of all Trades connected with Building,
&c ,&c. Edited by F T W. MILLER, Architect. Published Annually
3s 6d , half-bound, 4s

182 *Carpentry and Joinery*—THE ELEMENTARY PRIN-
CIPLES OF CARPENTRY Chiefly composed from the Standard
Work of THOMAS TREDGOLD, C.E With Additions, Alterations,
and Corrections from the Works of the most Recent Authorities,
and a TREATISE ON JOINERY by E WYNDHAM TARN, M A.
Fourth Edition, Revised and Extended, with numerous Illustrations. 3s 6d ‡

182*.*Carpentry and Joinery. Atlas* of 35 Plates to
Accompany the above. With Descriptive Letterpress. 4to, 6s

185. *The Complete Measurer ;* The Measurement of
Boards, Glass, &c , Unequal-sided, Square-sided, Octagonal-sided,
Round Timber and Stone, and Standing Timber, &c By RICHARD
HORTON Fifth Edition. 4s., strongly bound in leather, 5s.

187. *Hints to Young Architects.* By G. WIGHTWICK.
New Edition. By G. H. GUILLAUME. Illustrated. 3s 6d.‡

188. *House Painting, Graining, Marbling, and Sign*
Writing A Practical Manual of, with a Course of Elementary
Drawing for House-Painters, Sign-Writers, &c , and a Collection of
Useful Receipts By ELLIS A DAVIDSON Fourth Edition. With
Coloured Plates. 5s. cloth limp ; 6s. cloth boards.

189. *The Rudiments of Practical Bricklaying.* In
Six Sections· General Principles, Arch Drawing, Cutting and
Setting; Pointing, Paving, Tiling, Materials, Slating and Plaster-
ing ; Practical Geometry, Mensuration, &c By ADAM HAMMOND.
Fifth Edition. 1s 6d   [*Just published.*

191. *Plumbing.* A Text-Book to the Practice of the
Art or Craft of the Plumber. With Chapters upon House Drainage.
Fourth Edition. With 330 Illustrations. By W. P BUCHAN.
3s. 6d ‡

192. *The Timber Importer's, Timber Merchant's,* and
Builder's Standard Guide   By RICHARD E. GRANDY   Second
Edition, Revised   3s ‡

206. *A Book on Building, Civil and Ecclesiastical,*
including CHURCH RESTORATION With the Theory of Domes and
the Great Pyramid, &c By Sir EDMUND BECKETT, Bart., LL D.,
Q C , F.R.A S   4s. 6d.‡

226. *The Joints Made and Used by Builders* in the
Construction of various kinds of Engineering and Architectural
Works. By WYVILL J CHRISTY, Architect. With upwards of 160
Engravings on Wood. 3s.‡

228. *The Construction of Roofs of Wood and Iron.*
By E WYNDHAM TARN, M.A., Architect. Second Edition, Revised.
1s. 6d.

Architecture, Building, etc., *continued.*

2 9. *Elementary Decoration :* As applied to the Interior and Exterior Decoration of Dwelling-Houses, &c   By
James W Facey. Illustrated with Sixty eight Explanatory Engravings   2s

257. *Practical House Decoration :* A Guide to the
Art of Ornamental Painting, the Arrangement of Colours in Apart-
ments and the Principles of Decorative Design, &c   With
numerous Illustrations   2s 6d.   [*Just published.*

* Nos 229 *and* 257 *in One handsome Vol., half-bound, entitled "*House
Decoration, Elementary and Practical," *price* 5s.

230 *Handrailing.* By George Collings. With Plates
and Diagrams   1s 6d

247. *Building Estates :* A Rudimentary Treatise on the
Development, Sale, Purchase, and General Management of Building Land   By Fowler Maitland, Surveyor   Illustrated.   2s.

248. *Portland Cement for Users.* By Henry Faija,
Assoc M Inst C.E.   Second Edition, corrected. Illustrated   2s.

252. *Brickwork :* A Practical Treatise, embodying the
General and Higher Principles of Bricklaying, Cutting and Setting,
&c   By F. Walker.   Second Edition, Revised and Enlarged
1s. 6d.   [*Just published*

23. *The Practical Brick and Tile Book.* Comprising :
189. Brick and Tile Making, by E. Dobson, A I C E , Practical
Bricklaying, by A. Hammond, Brickwork, by F Walker.
252. 550 pp., with 270 Illustrations. 6s. Strongly half-bound
[*Just published.*

253. *The Timber Merchant's, Saw-Miller's, and Im-*
porter's *Freight-Book and Assistant.* By Wm Richardson With
a Chapter on Speeds of Saw-Mill Machinery, &c By M Powis
Bale, A M Inst C.E , and a London Price List for Timber and Deal
Sawing, &c , 1884. 3s.†

258. *Circular Work in Carpentry and Joinery :* A
Practical Treatise on Circular Work of Single and Double Cur-
vature. By George Collings, Author of " Handrailing," &c
With numerous Diagrams   2s 6d.   [*Just published.*

259. *Gas Fitting :* A Practical Handbook, treating of
every Description of Gas Laying and Fitting. By John Black.
With upwards of 120 Illustrations. 2s 6d   [*Just published.*

NAVAL ARCHITECTURE, NAVIGATION, etc.

51. *Naval Architecture.*   An Exposition of the
Elementary Principles of the Science, and their Practical Application to Naval Construction By J Peake Fifth Edition. 3s 6d †

53*.*Ships for Ocean and River Service,* Elementary
and Practical Principles of the Construction of   By H A. Sommer-
feldt, Surveyor of the Royal Norwegian Navy. 1s. 6d.

53**.*An Atlas of Engravings* to Illustrate the above.
Twelve large Folding Plates   Royal 4to, cloth, 7s. 6d.

NAVAL ARCHITECTURE, NAVIGATION, ETC , *continued.*

54. *Masting, Mast-Making, and Rigging of Ships,*
Rudimentary Treatise on   Also Tables of Spars, Rigging, Blocks ,
Chain, Wire, and Hemp Ropes, relative to every class of·Vessels
By ROBERT KIPPING, N A.   Fifteenth Edition   Illustrated   2s.‡

54*.*Iron Ship-Building.* With Practical Examples and
Details for the Use of Ship Owners and Ship Builders   By JOHN
GRANTHAM. Consulting Engineer and Naval Architect. 5th Edition,
with Additions   4s.

55. *The Sailor's Sea Book :* A Rudimentary Treatise
on Navigation   By JAMES GREENWOOD, B A   With numerous
Woodcuts and Coloured Plates   New and Enlarged Edition   By
W. H ROSSER   2s 6d ‡

80. *Marine Engines and Steam Vessels.* By ROBERT
MURRAY, C E , Principal Officer to the Board of Trade for the
East Coast of Scotland District   Eighth Edition, thoroughly
Revised, with Additions by the Author and by GEORGE CARLISLE,
C.E , Senior Surveyor to the Board of Trade, Liverpool. 4s. 6d.
limp, 5s cloth boards.   [*Just published.*

83*bis.The Forms of Ships and Boats :* Hints, Experi-
mentally Derived, on some of the Principles regulating Shipbuild-
ing   By W BLAND. Seventh Edition, revised, with numerous Illustrations and Models, 1s 6d

99. *Navigation and Nautical Astronomy,* in Theory
and Practice. By Prof J. R. YOUNG.   New Edition   2s 6d.

106. *Ships' Anchors,* a Treatise on.   By G. COTSELL,
N A. 1s 6s.

149. *Sails and Sail Making,* an Elementary Treatise
on   With Draughting, and the Centre of Effort of the Sails.   Also
Weights and Sizes of Ropes, Masting, Rigging, and Sails of Steam
Vessels, &c , &c   Eleventh Edition.   By ROBERT KIPPING, N.A ,
Sailmaker.   Illustrated, 2s. 6d ‡

155. *The Engineer's Guide to the Royal and Mercan-*
tile Navies   By a PRACTICAL ENGINEER   Revised by D. F.
M'CARTHY.   3s

55. *Practical Navigation.*   Consisting of The Sailor's
&   Sea Book, by JAMES GREENWOOD and W. H ROSSER, together
with the requisite Mathematical and Nautical Tables for the Work-
204.   ing of the Problems, by HENRY LAW, C E , and Professor J R.
YOUNG   With numerous Wood Engravings and Coloured Plates.
7s.   Strongly half-bound

AGRICULTURE, GARDENING, etc.

61*.*A Complete Ready Reckoner for the Admeasure-*
ment of Land &c. By A ARMAN   Second Edition, Revised and
Extended by C. NORRIS, Surveyor, Valuer, &c.   2s.

131. *Miller's, Corn Merchant's, and Farmer's Ready*
Reckoner   Second Edition, with a Price List of Modern Flour-Mill
Machinery, by W S HUTTON, C.E   2s.   [*Just published.*

AGRICULTURE, GARDENING, ETC , *continued.*

140. *Soils, Manures, and Crops.* (Vol. I. OUTLINES
OF MODERN FARMING.) By R. SCOTT BURN. Woodcuts. 2s.

141. *Farming and Farming Economy,* Notes, Historical and Practical, on. (Vol, II. OUTLINES OF MODERN FARMING)
By R. SCOTT BURN. 3s.

142 *Stock : Cattle, Sheep and Horses.* (Vol. III.
OUTLINES OF MODERN FARMING) By R. SCOTT BURN. Woodcuts
2s. 6d.

145. *Dairy, Pigs, and Poultry,* Management of the.
By R. SCOTT BURN. With Notes on the Diseases of Stock (Vol.
IV. OUTLINES OF MODERN FARMING) Woodcuts 2s.

146 *Utilization of Sewage, Irrigation, and Reclam-
ation of Waste Land.* (Vol V OUTLINES OF MODERN FARMING)
By R SCOTT BURN. Woodcuts 2s 6d.

** *Nos* 140-1-2-5-6, *in One Vol , handsomely half-bound, entitled* "OUT-
LINES OF MODERN FARMING " By ROBERT SCOTT BURN. *Price* 12s.

177. *Fruit Trees,* the Scientific and Profitable Culture
of From the French of DU BREUIL Revised by GEO GLENNY
187 Woodcuts. 3s. 6d.‡

198. *Sheep : The History, Structure, Economy, and
Diseases of.* By W C SPOONER, M R V C , &c. Fourth Edition,
Enlarged, Including Specimens of New and Improved Breeds
3s 6d ‡

201. *Kitchen Gardening made Easy.* By GEORGE M.
F GLENNY. Illustrated. 1s. 6d ‡

207. *Outlines of Farm Management, and the Organ-
isation of Farm Labour.* Treating of the General Work of the
Farm, Field and Live Stock, Contract Work, Labour, &c. By
R SCOTT BURN 2s. 6d ‡

208. *Outlines of Landed Estates Management :* Treating of the Varieties of Lands, Methods of Farming, Farm Buildings,
Irrigation, Drainage, &c By R SCOTT BURN. 2s 6d ‡

** *Nos* 207 *and* 208, *in One Vol , handsomely half-bound entitled* "OUT-
LINES OF LANDED ESTATES AND FARM MANAGEMENT." By R SCOTT BURN.
Price 6s.

209. *The Tree Planter and Plant Propagator.* A
Practical Manual on the Propagation of Forest Trees, Fruit Trees
Flowering Shrubs, Flowering Plants, &c. By SAMUEL WOOD.
2s ‡

210. *The Tree Pruner :* A Practical Manual on the
Pruning of Fruit Trees, including also their Training and Renova-
tion, also the Pruning of Shrubs, Climbers, and Flowering Plants
By SAMUEL WOOD. 2s ‡

** *Nos* 209 *and* 210, *in One Vol , handsomely half-bound, entitled* "THE
TREE PLANTER, PROPAGATOR, and PRUNER By SAMUEL WOOD. *Price* 5s

218 *The Hay and Straw Measurer :* Being New
Tables for the use of Auctioneers, Valuers, Farmers, Hay and
Straw Dealers, &c. By JOHN STEELE. Fourth Edition 2s.

MATHEMATICS, ARITHMETIC, etc.

32. *Mathematical Instruments,* A Treatise on; in
which their Construction and the Methods of Testing, Adjusting,
and Using them are concisely Explained By J F HEATHER,
M A , of the Royal Military Academy, Woolwich Original Edition,
in One Vol , Illustrated. 1s. 6d

* *In ordering the above, be careful to say "Original Edition" (No. 32), to distinguish it from the Enlarged Edition, in Three Vols (Nos 168-9 70).*

76. *Descriptive Geometry,* an Elementary Treatise
on. With a Theory of Shadows and of Perspective, extracted from
the French of G MONGE To which is added a Description of the
Principles and Practice of Isometrical Projection By J. F
HEATHER, M A. With 14 Plates. 2s.

178 *Practical Plane Geometry :* Giving the Simplest
Modes of Constructing Figures contained in one Plane and Geo-
metrical Construction of the Ground. By J F HEATHER, M A.
With 215 Woodcuts 2s.

83. *Commercial Book-keeping.* With Commercial
Phrases and Forms in English, French, Italian, and German By
JAMES HADDON, M A., Arithmetical Master of King's College School,
London, 1s. 6d

84. *Arithmetic,* A Rudimentary Treatise on. With full
Explanations of its Theoretical Principles, and numerous Examples for Practice By Professor J R. YOUNG. Tenth Edition,
corrected. 1s 6d

84*. A KEY to the above, containing Solutions in full to the Exercises, together with Comments, Explanations, and Improved Processes, for
the Use of Teachers and Unassisted Learners. By J. R. YOUNG.
1s. 6d.

85. *Equational Arithmetic,* Applied to Questions of
Interest, Annuities, Life Assurance, and General Commerce. With
various Tables by which all Calculations may be greatly Facilitated
By W. HIPSLEY 2s.

86. *Algebra,* The Elements of. By JAMES HADDON,
M A With Appendix, containing miscellaneous Investigations,
and a Collection of Problems in various parts of Algebra 2s

86*. A KEY AND COMPANION to the above Book, forming an extensive Re-
pository of Solved Examples and Problems in Illustration of the
various Expedients necessary in Algebraical Operations. By J R.
YOUNG. 1s 6d.

88. *Euclid,* The Elements of. With many additional
89. Propositions and Explacatory Notes To which is prefixed an In-
troductory Essay on Logic By HENRY LAW, C.E. 2s 6d.‡

* *Sold also separately, viz, —*

88. EUCLID. The First Three Books. By HENRY LAW, C E 1s 6d.
89. EUCLID. Books 4, 5, 6, 11, 12. By HENRY LAW, C E. 1s 6d.

90. *Analytical Geometry and Conic Sections..* By
JAMES HANN. A New Edition, by Professor J. R YOUNG. 2s.‡

MATHEMATICS, ARITHMETIC, ETC , *continued.*

91. *Plane Trigonometry,* The Elements of. By JAMES
HANN, formerly Mathematical Master of King's College, London.
1s. 6d

92. *Spherical Trigonometry,* The Elements of.   By
JAMES HANN. Revised by CHARLES H DOWLING, C E. 1s
`.·*` *Or with " The Elements of Plane Trigonometry," in One Volume, 2s 6d.*

93. *Mensuration and Measuring :* With the Mensuration and Levelling of Land for the Purposes of Modern Engineering. By T. BAKER, C E New Edition, by E NUGENT, C E.
Illustrated 1s. 6d

101. *Differential Calculus,* Elements of the. By W. S. B.
WOOLHOUSE, F R.A S , &c. 1s. 6d.

102. *Integral Calculus,* Rudimentary Treatise on the.
By HOMERSHAM COX, B A Illustrated 1s.

105. *Mnemonical Lessons.* —GEOMETRY, ALGEBRA, AND
TRIGONOMETRY, in Easy Mnemonical Lessons. By the Rev. THOMAS
PENYNGTON KIRKMAN, M.A. 1s. 6d.

136 *Arithmetic,* Rudimentary: For the use of Schools
and Self-Instruction By JAMES HADDON, M A Revised by A
ARMAN. 1s 6d.

137. A KEY TO HADDON'S RUDIMENTARY ARITHMETIC. By A ARMAN 1s 6d.

168. *Drawing and Measuring Instruments.* Including
—I. Instruments employed in Geometrical and Mechanical Draw-
ing, and in the Construction, Copying, and Measurement of Maps
and Plans   II. Instruments used for the purposes of Accurate
Measurement and for Arithmetical Computations. By J F.
HEATHER, M A. Illustrated. 1s 6d

169. *Optical Instruments.* Including (more especially)
Telescopes, Microscopes, and Apparatus for Producing Copies of
Maps and Plans by Photography. By J. F. HEATHER, M.A Illus-
trated   1s. 6d.

170. *Surveying and Astronomical Instruments.* In-
cluding—I Instruments used for Determining the Geometrical
Features of a Portion of Ground. II Instruments employed in
Astronomical Observations. By J F. HEATHER, M A. Illust 1s 6d

`*.*` *The above three volumes form an enlargement of the Author's original work,*
" Mathematical Instruments " (See No. 32 in the Series)

168. *Mathematical Instruments.* By J. F. HEATHER,
169.   M A. Enlarged Edition, for the most part entirely Re-written The
170.   Three Parts as above in One thick Volume. With numerous Illus-
        trations 4s. 6d ↓

158. *The Slide Rule, and How to Use it :* Containing
full, easy, and simple Instructions to Perform all Business Calculations with unexampled Rapidity and Accuracy. By CHARLES
HOARE, C.E. Fifth Edition. With a Slide Rule in tuck of cover.
2s 6d ↑

Mathematics, Arithmetic, etc., *continued.*

196. *Theory of Compound Interest and Annuities :*
With Tables of Logarithms for the more difficult Computations of Interest, Discount, Annuities, &c. By Fedor Thoman. 4s.‡

199. *The Compendious Calculator ;* or, Easy and Concise Methods of Performing the [various Arithmetical Operations required in Commercial and Business Transactions ; together with Useful Tables By D O'Gorman Twenty-sixth Edition, carefully Revised by C. Norris. 3s , cloth limp, 3s 6d., strongly halfbound in leather.

204. *Mathematical Tables :* For Trigonometrical, Astronomical, and Nautical Calculations To which is Prefixed a Treatise on Logarithms. By Henry Law, C E. Together with a Series of Tables for Navigation and Nautical Astronomy. By Professor J R. Young. New Edition. 4s ‡

204*.*Logarithms :* With Mathematical Tables for Trigonometrical, Astronomical, and Nautical Calculations. By Henry Law, M.Inst C.E. New and Revised Edition (forming part of the above Work). 3s.

221. *Measures, Weights, and Moneys of all Nations,* and an Analysis of the Christian, Hebrew, and Mahometan Calendars. By W S. B. Woolhouse, F.R.A.S, F.S S. Sixth Ed 2s ‡

227. *Mathematics as applied to the Constructive Arts.* Illustrating the various processes of Mathematical Investigation, by means of Arithmetical and Simple Algebraical Equations and Practical Examples. By Francis Campin, C E. Second Ed. 3s.‡

PHYSICAL SCIENCE, NATURAL PHILO-SOPHY, etc.

1. *Chemistry.* By Professor George Fownes, F.R.S. With an Appendix on the Application of Chemistry to Agriculture 1s

2. *Natural Philosophy,* Introduction to the Study of. By C. Tomlinson. Woodcuts. 1s. 6d.

6. *Mechanics,* Rudimentary Treatise on. By Charles Tomlinson. Illustrated. 1s. 6d.

7. *Electricity :* Showing the General Principles of Electrical Science, and the purposes to which it has been applied. By Sir W. Snow Harris, F.R.S, &c With Additions by R. Sabine, C.E., F S.A.

7.**Galvanism.* By Sir W. Snow Harris. New Edition, by Robert Sabine, C.E., F S.A. 1s. 6d.

8. *Magnetism :* Being a Concise Exposition of the General Principles of Magnetical Science. By Sir W. Snow Harris. New Edition, Revised by H. M. Noad, Ph.D. With 165 Woodcuts. 3s. 6d.‡

D

PHYSICAL SCIENCE, ETC., *continued.*

1. *The Electric Telegraph :* Its History and Progress; with Descriptions of some of the Apparatus. By R. SABINE, C E., F S A 3s.

12. *Pneumatics,* for the Use of Beginners. By CHARLES TOMLINSON. Illustrated 1s. 6d

72. *Manual of the Mollusca :* A Treatise on Recent and Fossil Shells By Dr S. P WOODWARD, A L S Fourth Edition With Appendix by RALPH TATE, A L S, F G S. With numerous Plates and 300 Woodcuts 6s. 6d, cloth boards, 7s. 6d

96. *Astronomy.* By the late Rev. ROBERT MAIN, M.A Third Edition, by WILLIAM THYNNE LYNN, B.A., F.R.A S. 2s.

97. *Statics and Dynamics,* the Principles and Practice of, embracing also a clear development of Hydiostatics, Hydrodynamics, and Central Forces. By T. BAKER, C E. 1s. 6d.

138. *Telegraph,* Handbook of the : A Guide to Candidates for Employment in the Telegraph Service By R. BOND. Fourth Edition. Including Questions on Magnetism, Electricity, and Practical Telegraphy, by W. McGREGOR. 3s.‡

173. *Physical Geology,* partly based on Major-General PORTLOCK's "Rudiments of Geology." By RALPH TATE, A.L.S., &c Woodcuts. 2s

174. *Historical Geology,* partly based on Major-General PORTLOCK's "Rudiments" By RALPH TATE, A L.S., &c. Woodcuts. 2s 6d

173 & 174. *Rudimentary Treatise on Geology,* Physical and Historical Partly based on Major-General PORTLOCK's "Rudiments of Geology." By RALPH TATE, A.L S , F.G.S., &c. In One Volume, 4s 6d.‡

183 & 184. *Animal Physics,* Handbook of. By Dr. LARDNER, D C L , formerly Professor of Natural Philosophy and Astronomy in University College, Lond With 520 Illustrations. In One Vol 7s 6d , cloth boards.

₊ *Sold also in Two Parts, as follows :—*

183 ANIMAL PHYSICS. By Dr LARDNER Part I , Chapters I.-VII. 4s.

184 ANIMAL PHYSICS. By Dr LARDNER Part II , Chapters VIII-XVIII. 3s

FINE ARTS.

20. *Perspective for Beginners.* Adapted to Young Students and Amateurs in Architecture, Painting, &c. By GEORGE PYNE. 2s.

40. *Glass Staining, and the Art of Painting on Glass.* From the German of Dr. GESSERT and EMANUEL OTTO FROMBERG With an Appendix on THE ART OF ENAMELLING. 2s. 6d.

69. *Music,* A Rudimentary and Practical Treatise on. With numerous Examples. By CHARLES CHILD SPENCER.

Fine Arts, *continued.*

71. *Pianoforte,* The Art of Playing the. With numerous
Exercises and Lessons from the Best Masters By Charles
Child Spencer. 1s 6d.

69-71. *Music and the Pianoforte.*   In One Vol.   Half
bound, 5s

181. *Painting popularly Explained,* including Fresco,
Oil, Mosaic, Water Colour, Water-Glass, Tempera, Encaustic,
Miniature, Painting on Ivory, Vellum, Pottery, Enamel, Glass, &c
With Historical Sketches of the Progress of the Art By Thomas
John Gullick, Assisted by John Timbs, F.S.A Fifth Edition,
revised and enlarged. 5s.‡

186. *A Grammar of Colouring,* applied to Decorative
Painting and the Arts. By George Field. New Edition, enlarged and adapted to the Use of the Ornamental Painter and
Designer. By Ellis A Davidson. With Two new Coloured Diagrams, &c. 3s.‡

246. *A Dictionary of Painters, and Handbook for*
Picture Amateurs, including Methods of Painting, Cleaning, Re-
lining and Restoring, Schools of Painting, &c. With Notes on the
Copyists and Imitators of each Master. By P Daryl. 2s. 6d ‡

INDUSTRIAL AND USEFUL ARTS.

23. *Bricks and Tiles,* Rudimentary Treatise on the
Manufacture of By E. Dobson, M R.I B A. Illustrated, 3s.‡

67. *Clocks, Watches, and Bells,* A Rudimentary
Treatise on By Sir Edmund Beckett, LL D , Q C. Seventh
Edition, revised and enlarged. 4s 6d limp , 5s. 6d cloth boards

83**. *Construction of Door Locks.*   Compiled from the
Papers of A C. Hobbs, and Edited by Charles Tomlinson, F R.S
With Additions by Robert Mallet, M I C.E. Illust 2s 6d.

162. *The Brass Founder's Manual :* Instructions for
Modelling, Pattern-Making, Moulding, Turning, Filing, Burnishing, Bronzing, &c With copious Receipts, &c By Walter Graham. 2s ‡

205. *The Art of Letter Painting made Easy.*   By
J G Badenoch. With 12 full-page Engravings of Examples. 1s.

215. *The Goldsmith's Handbook,* containing full Instructions, for the Alloying and Working of Gold. By G. E. Gee. 3s.‡

225. *The Silversmith's Handbook,* containing full Instructions for the Alloying and Working of Silver. By George E.
Gee. 3s.‡

** *The two preceding Works, in One handsome Vol., half-bound, entitled,*
"The Goldsmith's and Silversmith's Complete Handbook," 7s
[*Just published.*

224. *Coach Building,* A Practical Treatise, Historical
and Descriptive. By J. W. Burgess. 2s. 6d.‡

INDUSTRIAL AND USEFUL ARTS, *continued.*

235. *Practical Organ Building.* By W. E. DICKSON, M.A., Precentor of Ely Cathedral. Illustrated. 2s. 6d ‡

249. *The Hall-Marking of Jewellery Practically Considered.* By GEORGE E GEE. 3s ‡

MISCELLANEOUS VOLUMES.

36. *A Dictionary of Terms used in Architecture,* Building, Engineering, Mining, Metallurgy, Archæology, the Fine Arts, &c. By JOHN WEALE. Fifth Edition. Revised by ROBERT HUNT, F.R.S. Illustrated. 5s limp, 6s cloth boards.

50. *The Law of Contracts for Works and Services.* By DAVID GIBBONS. Third Edition, enlarged. 3s.‡

112. *Manual of Domestic Medicine.* By R. GOODING, B A , M D. Intended as a Family Guide in all Cases of Accident and Emergency. Third Edition. 2s.‡

112*.*Management of Health.* A Manual of Home and Personal Hygiene By the Rev. JAMES BAIRD, B.A 1s.

150. *Logic,* Pure and Applied. By S. H. EMMENS. 1s.6d.

153. *Selections from Locke's Essays on the Human Understanding.* With Notes by S. H. EMMENS. 2s.

154. *General Hints to Emigrants.* Notices of the various Fields for Emigration, Hints on Outfits, Useful Recipes, &c. 2s.

157. *The Emigrant's Guide to Natal.* By ROBERT JAMES MANN, F R A S , F M S. Second Edition Map 2s.

193. *Handbook of Field Fortification,* intended for the Guidance of Officers preparing for Promotion. By Major W. W. KNOLLYS, F.R.G S. With 163 Woodcuts 3s.‡

194. *The House Manager :* Being a Guide to Housekeeping, Practical Cookery, Pickling and Preserving, Household Work, Dairy Management, the Table and Dessert, Cellarage of Wines, Home-brewing and Wine-making, the Boudoir and Dressing-room, Travelling, Stable Economy, Gardening Operations, &c. By an OLD HOUSEKEEPER. 3s. 6d.‡

194. *The House Book.* Comprising : I. THE HOUSE
112   MANAGER. By an OLD HOUSEKEEPER. II. DOMESTIC MEDICINE.
and   By RALPH GOODING, M D III MANAGEMENT OF HEALTH. By
112*   JAMES BAIRD. In One Vol , strongly half-bound, 6s.

CROSBY LOCKWOOD & CO., 7, *Stationers' Hall Court, E C.*

J OGDEN AND CO LIMITED, PRINTERS, GREAT SAFFRON HILL, E C.

Lightning Source UK Ltd.
Milton Keynes UK
UKHW051427031022
409740UK00014B/80